FIELD GUIDES

AMPHIBIANS
Rachel Seigel

Abdo Reference

An Imprint of Abdo Publishing | abdobooks.com

CONTENTS

What Is an Amphibian? 4
How to Use This Book 6

Frogs

African Bullfrog 8
African Clawed Frog 9
Common Frog 10
Common Midwife Toad 11
Darwin's Frog 12
Dyeing Poison Dart Frog 13
Eastern Banjo Frog 14
Eastern Gray Tree Frog 15
Eastern Narrow-Mouthed Toad 16
Fleischmann's Glass Frog 17
Forest Green Treefrog 18
Giant Frog 19
Goliath Frog 20
Gottlebe's Narrow-Mouthed Frog ... 21
Gray Tree Frog 22
Green Frog 23
Green Tree Frog 24
Hairy Frog 25
Hip-Pocket Frog 26
Indus Valley Bullfrog 27
Lesueur's Frog 28
Marsh Frog 29
Mediterranean Painted Frog 30
Mexican Burrowing Toad 31
North American Bullfrog 32
Northern Cricket Frog 33
Northern Leopard Frog 34
Oriental Fire-Bellied Toad 35
Pacific Tailed Frog 36
Plains Spadefoot Toad 37
Puerto Rican Coquí 38
Pumpkin Toadlet 39
Purple Frog 40
Red-Eyed Treefrog 41
Riobamba Marsupial Frog 42
Smoky Jungle Frog 43
Strawberry Poison Frog..................... 44
Sumaco Horned Treefrog.................. 45
Surinam Horned Frog 46
Surinam Toad 47
Titicaca Water Frog 48
Turtle Frog 49
Tusked Frog 50
Vietnamese Mossy Frog 51
Wallace's Flying Frog 52
Western Green and
Golden Bell Frog 53
Wood Frog 54
Yellow-Bellied Toad 55

Toads

American Toad 56
Asiatic Toad 57
Cane Toad 58
Golden Toad 59
Guttural Toad 60
Mongolian Toad 61
Natterjack Toad 62
Panamanian Golden Frog 63
Red-Spotted Toad 64
Sambas Stream Toad 65
Southeast Asian Toad 66
Starry Night Harlequin Toad 67
Western Leopard Toad 68
Western Toad 69

Salamanders

Alpine Salamander 70
Axolotl 71
California Giant Salamander 72
Chinese Giant Salamander 73
Common Mudpuppy 74
Common Worm Salamander 75
Corsican Fire Salamander 76
Dwarf Salamander 77
Eastern Red-Backed Salamander .. 78
Fire Salamander 79
Georgia Blind Salamander 80
Gold-Striped Salamander 81
Hellbender 82
Japanese Clawed Salamander 83
Japanese Giant Salamander 84
Marbled Salamander 85
Nauta Mushroom-Tongue
Salamander 86
Olm 87
Reticulated Siren 88
Seal Salamander 89
Siberian Salamander 90
Splendid Moroccan Salamander 91
Tiger Salamander 92
Two-Toed Amphiuma 93

Newts

Algerian Ribbed Newt 94
California Newt 95
Chinese Warty Newt 96
Eastern Newt 97
Great Crested Newt 98
Himalayan Newt 99
Lorestan Newt 100
Rough-Skinned Newt 101
Smooth Newt 102
Spanish Newt 103

Caecilians

Congo Caecilian 104
Kirk's Caecilian 105
Ringed Caecilian 106
Rio Cauca Caecilian 107

Glossary 108
To Learn More 109
Photo Credits 110

WHAT IS AN AMPHIBIAN?

Amphibians evolved from fish more than 340 million years ago. Amphibians live on both water and land, and they are vertebrates, meaning they have backbones. These creatures have evolved to survive in multiple habitats. These range from hot deserts to ponds and streams to arctic tundra. Amphibians are found everywhere in the world except for Antarctica. Many amphibian species undergo metamorphosis. This means the amphibian drastically changes form as it ages. Other species undergo direct development. This means the amphibian starts life as a miniature version of its adult form. Most amphibians are carnivores, meaning that they eat animals or insects. Some are herbivores, eating only plants. Others are omnivores and eat both.

WHAT ARE AMPHIBIANS LIKE?

There are three main groups of amphibians: frogs, salamanders, and caecilians. There are thousands of known amphibian species. More are discovered every year. Amphibians vary in size and appearance. But there are some traits they have in common.

- All amphibians are ectotherms. This means they need external sources, such as the sun, to heat their bodies.

- All amphibians have thin, soft, moist skin that helps them breathe.

   Frogs are one of the most diverse types of amphibians in the world. There are more than 7,000 known frog species, but they all share specific traits. Frogs usually have four legs of unequal size. Their back legs are long. This helps them jump. Toads are a type of frog. Toads usually have dry, warty skin. They are poisonous. There is only one family of true toads. Some frogs have an incorrect common name of *toad*.

Salamanders have long, slim bodies and long tails. Most salamanders have four legs, while some have two. There are more than 700 known salamander species. They live all over the world, but the largest number of salamander families are found in North America. Salamanders are nocturnal, meaning they come out at night to eat. Newts are a type of salamander that spend most of their time on land. They have dry, bumpy skin. Sirens are another type of salamander. They spend most of their time in the water.

Caecilians are tropical, limbless, worm-like amphibians. There are 200 known caecilian species. Their skin is shiny and has ringed folds of skin called annuli. Caecilians come in a variety of colors, including gray, black, orange, or yellow. Some have tiny scales in their rings. Some caecilians live in the water, but most are burrowers. This means they dig and live in underground tunnels. They have tiny eyes that are hidden under their skin or skulls. Caecilians also don't have ear openings. They don't hear sound the way that humans do.

WHAT ROLE DO AMPHIBIANS PLAY?

Amphibians play a key role in the ecosystem as both predators and prey. They get their energy from eating plants and other animals. This makes them important to the food chain. Many amphibians eat insects that carry diseases, such as mosquitoes, or that can harm crops. They are also food for other species, including fish, birds, mammals, insects, and other amphibians.

HOW TO USE THIS BOOK

Tab shows the amphibian category.

TOADS

SOUTHEAST ASIAN TOAD
(DUTTAPHRYNUS MELANOSTICTUS)

The amphibian's common name appears here.

Southeast Asian toads are one of the most common toads in Asia. They are medium-large with small heads. Their color ranges from gray to reddish brown, yellow, or pale yellow brown with black markings. The toads' backs are covered in spiny warts with dark spots. Their heads have black, bony ridges above their eyes. Southeast Asian toads are poor climbers and can't jump very high.

HOW TO SPOT

How to Spot features give information on how to identify the amphibian.

Size: 2.2 to 3.3 inches (5.7 to 8.3 cm) long from snout to vent
Range: South and Southeast Asia and southern China
Habitat: Tropical and subtropical forests
Diet: Insects

FUN FACT
Southeast Asian toads are invasive in Madagascar. Scientists believe they accidentally arrived there in shipping containers.

Fun Facts give interesting information related to the amphibian.

6

STARRY NIGHT HARLEQUIN TOAD (ATELOPUS ARYECUE...)

Starry night harlequin toads are a critically endangered species. In 2019, scientists rediscovered them after not having seen them since 1991. Starry night harlequin toads are shiny black with white spots. Their name comes from the clear, starry night skies in their habitat. They have slim bodies and pointy snouts. Their toes are pointed. Most harlequin toads are endangered. Conservationists are working to protect them and their habitats.

HOW TO...

Size: Und... long from ...
Range: Si... Santa Mar... range in Colombia
Habitat: Forests, wetlands, and grasslands
Diet: Invertebrates

SACRED TOADS

The Arhuaco people of Colombia have a special relationship with the starry night harlequin toad. The people consider the toads, called *gouna*, to be sacred. The people rely on the toads' singing to indicate when to plant crops. The Arhuaco people worked closely with conservationists to allow scientists to study starry night toads in a way that respected their habitat and Arhuaco culture.

FROGS

AFRICAN BULLFROG
(PYXICEPHALUS ADSPERSUS)

African bullfrogs are the largest frog species in sub-Saharan Africa. They are the second-largest known frog species in the world. Adult African bullfrogs have round bodies and olive-green skin. Males have a yellow or orange throat, and females have cream-colored throats. Due to the extreme temperatures in their environments, African bullfrogs spend as much as ten months of the year hibernating underground. When the rainy season begins, they wake up from hibernation and gather in groups to look for mates.

HOW TO SPOT

Size: 4.5 to 10 inches (11.4 to 25.4 cm) long from snout to vent
Range: Central, eastern, and southern Africa
Habitat: Open grasslands
Diet: Snakes, insects, rodents, birds, small mammals, and other amphibians

FUN FACT
African bullfrogs are extremely aggressive. Males have large tusks in their mouths. They attack intruders to their habitat.

Female

AFRICAN CLAWED FROG
(XENOPUS LAEVIS)

African clawed frogs have flattened bodies with smooth skin. Their eyes and nostrils are on top of their small, wedge-shaped heads. They usually have brown or greenish-gray backs. Their undersides are off-white with yellow tones. An African clawed frog can change its appearance, becoming lighter, darker, or spotted to match its background. Its front limbs are small with unwebbed fingers. African clawed frogs use their long fingers to put food in their mouths. Their back legs are large with webbed toes. Three of their five toes on each back foot have claw-like tips. African clawed frogs are excellent swimmers, but they are awkward on land. They crawl instead of hopping.

HOW TO SPOT

Size: 2 to 4.5 inches (5.1 to 11.4 cm) long from snout to vent
Range: Eastern and southern Africa and parts of western Africa
Habitat: Quiet streams and warm, still ponds
Diet: Invertebrates, small fish, and almost anything else that crosses their paths

FROGS

COMMON FROG (RANA TEMPORARIA)

Common frogs are also known as European common frogs or European brown frogs. These frogs can be found as far north as the Arctic Circle in Scandinavia. They have flat heads with rounded snouts, thickset bodies, and smooth, moist skin. Common frogs are usually gray, brown, or olive green but can occasionally be red or yellow. Common frogs often have a dark patch behind their eyes like a mask and dark stripes on their back legs. They have powerful legs that they use for jumping and swimming. They mostly live on land but breed in water.

HOW TO SPOT

Size: 2.4 to 3.5 inches (6 to 9 cm) long from snout to vent

Range: British Isles, Europe, and northwestern Asia

Habitat: Areas that are close to fresh water and stay damp in the summer; commonly found in garden ponds, puddles, lakes, and canals

Diet: Slugs, snails, and other invertebrates

FUN FACT

Like most frogs, common frogs drink by absorbing water through their skin. They swallow by pulling their eyes back into their heads to push the food down.

COMMON MIDWIFE TOAD
(ALYTES OBSTETRICANS)

Common midwife toads are not really toads. They are frogs with warty skin and thick bodies like toads. They are usually gray or brown. They have olive, green, black, or brown spots on the throat and chest. They have whitish undersides. Red warts usually cover their bodies. Common midwife toads live primarily on land as adults and only live in water as tadpoles. They are nocturnal and feed at night. During the day, they hide under logs or dig holes to stay moist.

HOW TO SPOT

Size: 1 to 2 inches (2.5 to 5 cm) long from snout to vent
Range: Western Europe and the United Kingdom
Habitat: Farmlands, forests, and wetlands
Diet: Insects and other invertebrates

Male

CARRYING THE EGGS

Common midwife toads are known for their unique way of parenting. The males carry strings of fertilized eggs wrapped around their back legs for up to six weeks. When the eggs are ready to hatch, the male drops them into water.

FROGS

DARWIN'S FROG
(RHINODERMA DARWINII)

Darwin's frogs have skin that is usually green, brown, or both. Their undersides have patterns of black and white colorings. Darwin's frogs have triangular heads with long, pointy noses. They also have thin legs. A Darwin's frog catches prey by waiting for it to approach. Then the frog uses its long, sticky tongue to capture the prey. This frog is also nicknamed the "cowboy frog." This is because of the pattern of cow-like black-and-white spots on its underside.

FUN FACT
Darwin's frogs don't raise their young in water like most frogs. Instead, the male gathers the tadpoles in his vocal sac. They develop there, and after six weeks they emerge as tiny frogs.

HOW TO SPOT
Size: 1 to 1.4 inches (2.5 to 3.5 cm) long from snout to vent
Range: Argentina and Chile
Habitat: Rain forests and temperate forests
Diet: Insects and other land invertebrates

DYEING POISON DART FROG
(DENDROBATES TINCTORIUS)

Dyeing poison dart frogs have bright-blue skin. Some individuals have two wide yellow stripes on their heads and backs. Their arms and legs are deep blue and have several yellow or black spots. They are also called the blue poison dart frog because of their blue coloring. These frogs have no webbing on their toes and are poor swimmers. Because of this, they spend their time on land. The frog's bright color warns predators that it is poisonous. The toxins in its skin come from the food that it eats.

HOW TO SPOT

Size: 1.5 to 2 inches (3.8 to 5.1 cm) long from snout to vent

Range: French Guinea and northeastern Brazil

Habitat: Wet, fallen leaves on rain forest floors; sometimes in trees

Diet: Small spiders; ants, termites, and other small insects

LEGENDARY FROG

The name *dyeing poison dart frog* comes from legends that say Indigenous peoples of the Guianas and the Amazon used the frogs to dye parrot feathers. They would use the frog or a mixture of its skin and blood. They would rub it on a parrot's green feathers. After being plucked, legend says the feathers would grow back red or yellow.

FROGS

EASTERN BANJO FROG
(LIMNODYNASTES DUMERILII)

Eastern banjo frogs are large, warty frogs with thick, short legs and round heads. They range from pale gray to dark gray and have dark-bronze markings on their sides. Eastern banjo frogs are burrowing frogs. They are primarily seen after rainfall. They have a shovel-like growth on their hind toes to help with burrowing. The eastern banjo frog makes a *bonk* sound. It sounds like the plucking of a banjo string. The chorus of *bonk bonks* together led to the nickname "pobblebonk."

FUN FACT
There are five subspecies of eastern banjo frogs, each found in different parts of Australia. They all have slightly different color patterns and calls.

HOW TO SPOT

Size: Up to 3 inches (7.5 cm) long from snout to vent
Range: Tasmania and southeastern Australia
Habitat: Grasslands, wetlands, and river areas
Diet: Small invertebrates

EASTERN GRAY TREE FROG
(HYLA VERSICOLOR)

Eastern gray tree frogs aren't only gray. They also have green or brown colorings, and they can be solid or have spots on their backs. The word *versicolor* in their scientific name is Latin for "variable color." This refers to the frog's ability to lighten or darken its skin depending on the time of day and the temperature. The undersides of their legs are bright yellow or orange. Sticky mucus from their skin helps them climb up or across trees and stick to surfaces. Eastern gray tree frogs are nocturnal. They hide under leaves, tree roots, and rotten logs during the day.

HOW TO SPOT

Size: Males 1.3 to 2 inches (3.3 to 5.1 cm) long from snout to vent; females 1.5 to 2.3 inches (3.8 to 5.8 cm) long
Range: Eastern United States and southeastern Canada
Habitat: Wooded habitats such as forests, swamps, farms, and backyards where there is access to trees and water
Diet: Different types of insects, spiders, plant mites, snails, slugs, and occasionally smaller frogs

FROGS

EASTERN NARROW-MOUTHED TOAD *(GASTROPHRYNE CAROLINENSIS)*

Despite its name, the eastern narrow-mouthed toad is a frog, not a toad. It has a plump body similar to a toad. Eastern narrow-mouthed toads can be light tan, brown, red, or almost black. The middle of the back is covered by light or dark patches and spots, and the underside is heavily spotted. They have short legs with no webbing between the toes. A flap of skin runs behind the eastern narrow-mouthed toad's eyes. The frog can fold the flap of skin forward. This keeps insects out of its eyes.

HOW TO SPOT

Size: 1 to 1.5 inches (2.5 to 3.8 cm) long from snout to vent

Range: Southeastern North America

Habitat: Anywhere there is moisture and shelter, but often found in woodland habitats

Diet: Invertebrates, especially ants

FLEISCHMANN'S GLASS FROG
(HYALINOBATRACHIUM FLEISCHMANNI)

Fleischmann's glass frogs have semitransparent skin on their bellies. This makes the heart and other organs visible. The rest of the frog is pale green with yellow dots. Fleischmann's glass frogs have short snouts and gold irises. Their fingers and toes have small yellow suction pads. Fleischmann's glass frogs spend their days hiding under leaves and in branches. At night, they come out of hiding to hunt for food and look for mates. The females lay their eggs on the undersides of leaves or on branches found near running water. After hatching, the tadpoles fall into the water below, where they develop.

HOW TO SPOT

Size: 0.9 to 1 inches (2.2 to 2.5 cm) long from snout to vent

Range: Mexico, Central America, and South America

Habitat: Rain forests

Diet: Small insects, spiders, and other small invertebrates

FUN FACT

Male glass frogs watch over their eggs. They protect the eggs from predators and urinate on them to keep them moist. Only 10 percent of frog species care for their young.

FROGS

FOREST GREEN TREEFROG
(ZHANGIXALUS ARBOREUS)

Forest green treefrogs spend most of the year in trees or under piles of leaves. They hibernate in winter. Forest green treefrogs are bright green and sometimes have brown or black spots. There are brown marks on their chests and throats, and their undersides are white or cream-colored. Their backs and heads are covered with small bumps. Forest green treefrogs have large heads with orange-brown eyes. There is a ridge on each side of the head from the end of the snout to the eyes. They have webbed front toes and slightly webbed back toes.

HOW TO SPOT

Size: Males 1.7 to 2.4 inches (4.2 to 6 cm) long from snout to vent; females 2.3 to 3.2 inches (5.9 to 8.2 cm) long
Range: Honshu Island, Japan, and the nearby island Sado
Habitat: Lowland and mountainous forests
Diet: Insects

GIANT FROG (CYCLORANA AUSTRALIS)

Giant frogs are large frogs that live on land. They are also known as the northern snapping frog. The giant frog has a large, triangle-shaped head and horizontal pupils with gold irises. Giant frogs have tough, muscular bodies with long limbs. They have brown or bright-green backs. A dark stripe starts at the snout and continues down the frog's sides. Sometimes the frog will have a pale, thin, vertical stripe along its back. The frog's underside is white, and a male will have dark spots on its throat. The backs of the frog's thighs have brown patterns. Its toes are partially webbed.

HOW TO SPOT

Size: 3.1 to 3.9 inches (8 to 10 cm) long from snout to vent
Range: Northern Australia
Habitat: Grasslands and open woodlands
Diet: Likely invertebrates such as scorpions, spiders, ants, and centipedes

Male

FUN FACT
Giant frogs are one of the most commonly encountered frog species in northern Australia.

FROGS

GOLIATH FROG (CONRAUA GOLIATH)

Goliath frogs are the largest living frogs in the world and can get as large as a house cat. Goliath frogs are nocturnal. They sit on rocks at night and look for food. They have bumpy skin with glands that they use to drink water and get oxygen. Their backs are usually brownish green with spots. Their undersides are usually yellowish green or yellowish orange. These frogs are excellent jumpers and can leap forward distances of up to 10 feet (3 m).

HOW TO SPOT

Size: 6.7 to 12.6 inches (17 to 32 cm) long from snout to vent

Range: Cameroon and Equatorial Guinea

Habitat: Near rivers and waterfalls

Diet: Insects, crustaceans, fish, and other amphibians

FUN FACT

Goliath frogs attach their eggs to vegetation or stones underwater. Sometimes they make nests. They have been known to move rocks that are half their weight to build nests for their tadpoles.

GOTTLEBE'S NARROW-MOUTHED FROG
(SCAPHIOPHRYNE GOTTLEBEI)

Gottlebe's narrow-mouthed frogs are sometimes called Malagasy rainbow frogs or painted burrowing frogs. This is because of their unique color patterns. Their backs have a red area in the center with black, white, and green coloring around it. These frogs have white legs and lower bellies. They have short, strong limbs and webbed back feet. Horny points of bone on the bottoms of their back feet look like shovels and allow them to burrow. Claws on their front feet help them climb rocky canyon walls.

HOW TO SPOT

Size: 0.8 to 1.6 inches (2 to 4 cm) long from snout to vent
Range: Isalo Massif in southwestern Madagascar
Habitat: Narrow canyons
Diet: Insects and small invertebrates

FUN FACT

Gottlebe's narrow-mouthed frogs are poor swimmers because of their short legs. In addition, they have webbing only on their back feet.

FROGS

GRAY TREE FROG
(CHIROMANTIS XERAMPELINA)

Gray tree frogs can be pale green, brown, or gray. They have slightly bumpy skin with a pattern of light brown spots and lines across their backs and legs. Gray tree frogs spend a lot of time sitting in the hot sun. When their skin is exposed to sunlight, it turns white. This prevents their bodies from heating up and losing water. Male gray tree frogs whip up a foam with their back legs to create a nest for eggs. For this reason, they are also called gray foam nesting frogs.

Tadpoles in foam nest

HOW TO SPOT

Size: 2 to 3.5 inches (5 to 9 cm) long from snout to vent
Range: Eastern and southern Africa
Habitat: Savannas, shrublands, forests, and grasslands
Diet: Large insects

FUN FACT
Gray tree frogs have toe pads at the tip of each toe to help them climb trees.

GREEN FROG *(LITHOBATES CLAMITANS)*

Green frogs are sometimes mistaken for American bullfrogs and mink frogs. However, there are two dark ridges down their backs that set them apart. The ridges stick up slightly from the skin. Green frogs can be shades of green, brown, blue, or all three. They have green upper lips and spotted white bellies. They have large eardrums next to their eyes. In males, these are larger than their eyes. The green frog makes a *gunk* sound. It sounds like loose banjo strings being plucked.

HOW TO SPOT

Size: 3 to 4.9 inches (7.5 to 12.5 cm) long from snout to vent

Range: Eastern half of the United States and Canada

Habitat: Found near shallow, permanent water such as springs, brooks, ponds, and the edges of lakes

Diet: Slugs, spiders, and smaller frogs

Male

Female

FROGS

GREEN TREE FROG
(LITORIA CAERULEA)

Green tree frogs have smooth green skin with scattered white spots on their backs. Their bellies are creamy white with a rough texture. Their eyes are gold. A fold of fat over their eyes makes them look sleepy. They have flat toes with sticky surfaces made up of connected discs. These help green tree frogs to grip, allowing them to climb trees. During dry periods, green tree frogs cover their skin in a waxy coating to hold water.

HOW TO SPOT

Size: 3 to 4 inches (7.6 to 10.1 cm) long from snout to vent
Range: Australia, Indonesia, and Papua New Guinea
Habitat: Humid forests, woodlands, and urban areas
Diet: Insects, mice, and bats

FUN FACT

Like most frogs, green tree frogs regularly shed their skin to protect against bacteria. They eat discarded skin for its nutrients.

HAIRY FROG
(TRICHOBATRACHUS ROBUSTUS)

Hairy frogs have large, heavy bodies with small lungs. Their name comes from the hair-like skin fibers and arteries that males develop on their bodies during breeding season. Scientists believe that the growths help the frogs absorb more oxygen. The growths may also protect hairy frogs in fights with others of their species. Hairy frogs have long toes on their back feet. The frogs are greenish brown to black. They have a long, dark streak down their backs and small, dark spots near their backsides.

HOW TO SPOT

Size: 4.3 inches (11 cm) long from snout to vent
Range: Western Africa
Habitat: Tropical forests, wetlands
Diet: Grasshoppers, beetles, spiders, and slugs

Hairy growths develop during breeding season and are only used when the frog is in water.

WOLVERINE FROG

The hairy frog is also called the wolverine or horror frog. It has a unique defensive behavior. It will break its own toe bones, pushing the bones through the toes like claws when threatened. When the danger has passed, scientists believe the bones pull back into the skin and the damage to the toes heals.

FROGS

HIP-POCKET FROG
(ASSA DARLINGTONI)

Hip-pocket frogs are also called pouched frogs. The male has a pouch above the hind legs that is big enough to hold tadpoles. Hip-pocket frogs are brown or black with dark markings. They have a dark-brown stripe starting behind the eyes, going over the shoulder and onto the side behind their front legs. Their underside is white with brown spots. Their feet have unwebbed toes. Hip-pocket frogs commonly hide under piles of leaves, rocks, or other items on the forest floor where they can stay out of view.

FUN FACT
Hip-pocket frogs lay clumps of eight to 18 eggs on land. The male frog stays near the eggs. When the eggs hatch, five to nine tadpoles wriggle into the frog's pouches. The tadpoles develop in the pouches and emerge as fully formed small frogs.

HOW TO SPOT

Size: Up to 0.8 inches (2 cm) long from snout to vent
Range: Eastern Australia
Habitat: Subtropical forests
Diet: Mites, ants, and other invertebrates

INDUS VALLEY BULLFROG
(HOPLOBATRACHUS TIGERINUS)

Indus Valley bullfrogs are the largest frog species in the Pakistani plains. They have long heads and pointy snouts. Their yellow to olive-green coloring helps them camouflage. During mating season, the male changes color. He becomes bright yellow with large, bright-blue sacs under the jaw to attract females. Indus Valley bullfrogs are considered an invasive species on the islands of Andaman and Nicobar. They will eat almost anything that fits into their mouths. Indus Valley bullfrogs catch prey by pouncing on it and swallowing. They can also use their front limbs to push larger food into their mouths.

HOW TO SPOT

Size: Up to 6.5 inches (16.5 cm) long from snout to vent

Range: Afghanistan, Pakistan, India, Nepal, Bangladesh, and Myanmar

Habitat: Mainly aquatic, found mostly in freshwater wetlands

Diet: Invertebrates, small mammals, and birds

Male

FUN FACT
When they sense danger, Indus Valley bullfrogs dive into deep water and stay there for two to three minutes before returning to land.

FROGS

LESUEUR'S FROG *(LITORIA LESUEURI)*

Lesueur's frogs are usually seen at night. They are medium-sized frogs with gray-brown or reddish-brown backs. They sometimes have black marks on their backs. A black stripe runs from the eye to the front leg. The underside is white. The backs of their thighs and groin are black with blue patches. They have horizontal pupils. The iris is gold above the pupil and brown below. Lesueur's frogs have unwebbed fingers, but their toes are mostly webbed. In the early spring through late fall, males call to females from the sides of streams and ponds by making soft purring sounds.

HOW TO SPOT

Size: 1.8 to 2.8 inches (4.5 to 7 cm) long from snout to vent
Range: Eastern Australia
Habitat: Rocky or sandy streams in rain forests and tropical forests
Diet: Insects and other invertebrates

MARSH FROG *(PELOPHYLAX RIDIBUNDUS)*

Marsh frogs are the largest native frogs in Europe. They have large heads and long legs. They vary in color and are usually green or brown. They have two raised ridges starting behind their eyes that run down their backs. Their long back legs make them excellent jumpers, and their webbed feet help them swim. Marsh frogs are active during the day and at night. They will often bask in the sun.

HOW TO SPOT

Size: Up to 6.7 inches (17 cm) long from snout to vent

Range: Throughout Europe and into the Middle East and Russia

Habitat: Ponds, lakes, and rivers

Diet: Dragonflies, insects, spiders, slugs, small rodents, fish, and smaller amphibians

FUN FACT
Marsh frog calls sound like laughter. They produce the call from vocal sacs on either side of their mouths, which helps the sound carry for hundreds of yards.

FROGS

MEDITERRANEAN PAINTED FROG *(DISCOGLOSSUS PICTUS)*

Mediterranean painted frogs are small frogs with wide, flat heads. They usually have gray-green bodies and can vary in pattern. Some Mediterranean painted frogs are mostly one color. Others have large, dark spots with bright outlines. Some have alternating dark-brown and brightly colored bands. The frogs' pupils are shaped like upside-down tears. Mediterranean painted frogs are burrowers. They dig dens under stones, where they hide during the day.

HOW TO SPOT

Size: 2.7 to 2.8 inches (6.8 to 7 cm) long from snout to vent

Range: France, Italy, Malta, Spain, Morocco, Algeria, and Tunisia

Habitat: Coastal areas, woods, dry and humid forests; breeds in still and running water, including human-made water sources such as canals and pipes

Diet: Insects and other invertebrates

MEXICAN BURROWING TOAD
(RHINOPHRYNUS DORSALIS)

Mexican burrowing toads are dark brown to black with a reddish-orange stripe running down the center of their backs. Their skin has orange spots. Their bodies are round. The frogs' heads are small and triangular. Their snouts are covered in small, bumpy growths. Their feet have short, spade-like toes made from the same material as human nails. These help them dig. When the Mexican Burrowing toad is calling or scared, its body becomes inflated like a flattened balloon with a snout sticking out of one side.

FUN FACT
Mexican burrowing toads use their snouts to probe into termite and ant nests. Their tongues are attached at the back of the mouth instead of the front. This means that unlike most frogs, their tongues are projected out instead of flipped out.

HOW TO SPOT

Size: 2 to 2.8 inches (5.1 to 7.1 cm) long from snout to vent

Range: Southern Texas, Mexico, and Central America

Habitat: Tropical forests, savannas, land with low trees and bushes, anywhere with loose soil for burrowing

Diet: Ants, termites, and other insects and invertebrates

FROGS

NORTH AMERICAN BULLFROG
(LITHOBATES CATESBEIANUS)

North American bullfrogs are the largest frogs in North America. They are light to dark green or greenish brown. Their backs and sides are plain or have dark spots, and their arms and legs have dark spots. They have white undersides and golden or reddish-bronze eyes. North American bullfrogs are powerful swimmers, with strong back legs and large webbed feet. They can leap 6 feet (1.8 m), which is up to ten times their body length. North American bullfrogs are a highly invasive species. They have very few predators, and they will eat anything that will fit into their mouths.

HOW TO SPOT

Size: 6 to 8 inches (15.2 to 20.3 cm) long from snout to vent
Range: North America; introduced in South America, Europe, and Asia
Habitat: Lakes, ponds, rivers, and bogs
Diet: Crayfish, water beetles, snails, dragonfly larvae, fish, small turtles, young water birds, and other smaller frogs

FUN FACT
The North American bullfrog's deep call sounds like the mooing of a cow or bull. This is where the frog gets its name.

NORTHERN CRICKET FROG
(ACRIS CREPITANS)

Northern cricket frogs are small, rough-skinned frogs with skinny waists, long hind legs, and slim webbed toes. Their bodies are greenish brown, yellow, red, or black. There is a dark triangle patch between the eyes. Northern cricket frogs are part of the tree frog family, but they don't climb trees. Northern cricket frogs jump in zigzag patterns to avoid predators. They are active during the day and at night in warm weather. They are inactive in cold weather.

HOW TO SPOT

Size: 0.8 to 1.5 inches (2 to 3.8 cm) long from snout to vent

Range: Eastern and central United States and northeastern Mexico

Habitat: Ponds and streams with plants growing above the surface of the water

Diet: Insects, including mosquitoes

FROGS

NORTHERN LEOPARD FROG
(LITHOBATES PIPIENS)

Northern leopard frogs are a common species in North America, and they can survive both on land and in water. Adult northern leopard frogs are green or brown with white bellies. They have dark, rounded, leopard-like spots. Northern leopard frogs are also called meadow frogs because they are commonly found in meadows. They hunt in meadows and grasslands in the summer. They get water by absorbing dew from plants. Northern leopard frogs spend the winter in the mud and rotting leaves at the bottoms of their home ponds.

FUN FACT
Northern leopard frogs rely on their ability to jump quickly into the water or squawk and make uneven hops to escape predators. If they are captured, they will usually let out a loud scream.

HOW TO SPOT

Size: 2 to 4.4 inches (5 to 11.1 cm) long from snout to vent

Range: Northern part of North America and the southwestern United States

Habitat: Near water in marshlands and forests

Diet: Invertebrates and smaller frogs

ORIENTAL FIRE-BELLIED TOAD
(BOMBINA ORIENTALIS)

Oriental fire-bellied toads are aquatic frogs. They are covered in rough warts and range from brownish gray to grayish green to bright green, with dark spots or ridges. Their bellies are smooth. Red-orange or yellow spots are marbled with dark spots. Oriental fire-bellied toads have small heads with large eyes, and their pupils are triangle-shaped. Unlike other frogs and toads, oriental fire-bellied toads are unable to stick out their tongues to catch prey. Instead, they leap forward and catch food in their mouths.

HOW TO SPOT

Size: 1.4 to 3.1 inches (3.5 to 8 cm) long from snout to vent
Range: North Korea, South Korea, China, and Russia
Habitat: Still and running water in forests, bushlands, river valleys, and meadows
Diet: Insects, worms, and mollusks

WARNING!
When threatened, the oriental fire-bellied toad arches its body, revealing its brightly colored belly. These colors warn predators that the frog is poisonous. If attacked, the frog releases a toxin from glands on its body. The toxin irritates the attacker's mouth and nose.

FROGS

PACIFIC TAILED FROG
(ASCAPHUS TRUEI)

Pacific tailed frogs are small. They are typically reddish brown, olive green, black, or yellow. Their color matches the rocks where they live. They have rough skin and hardened claw-like fingertips. This allows them to move easily around the rocks and fast-moving water. There is a triangle on the nose and a dark stripe along the eye. Males have a tail-like extension of the cloaca that is used to reproduce.

HOW TO SPOT

Size: 0.9 to 2 inches (2.2 to 5.1 cm) long from snout to vent

Range: Coastal mountains of British Columbia, Canada; west coast of the United States

Habitat: Streams with clear, fast-moving water, rocky bottoms with little vegetation, and dense forest coverings

Diet: Insects, land invertebrates, and mollusks

Male

QUIET FROGS

Pacific tailed frogs do not have vocal sacs or external eardrums. These features are needed to make and hear sound. Scientists think these frogs communicate through sight and touch instead of sound.

PLAINS SPADEFOOT TOAD
(SPEA BOMBIFRONS)

Plains spadefoot toads are small frogs that resemble toads. Their bodies are gray, brown, or olive green, with darker spots and blotches. Four light lines run down their backs, and their undersides are white. Their skin is covered in small bumps. Their eyes are golden yellow with vertical pupils. Between the eyes is a bony lump. Their snouts are short and slightly upturned. Males have gray to bluish throats. Plains spadefoot toads have short legs and webbed feet. A black ridge called a spade at the bottom of each hind foot is the frog's namesake. The frogs use these spades for burrowing.

HOW TO SPOT

Size: 1.5 to 2.5 inches (3.8 to 6.4 cm) long from snout to vent

Range: Prairie regions of Canada, Great Plains of the United States, and northern Mexico

Habitat: Grasslands and areas with loose, sandy soil

Diet: Invertebrates such as beetles, ants, and worms

FUN FACT

Plains spadefoot toads hibernate underground in winter. They go below where the ground freezes. They can dig these burrows themselves or use mammal burrows.

FROGS

PUERTO RICAN COQUÍ
(ELEUTHERODACTYLUS COQUI)

Puerto Rican coquís are small tree frogs. They are a cultural symbol of Puerto Rico. These frogs are brown with tan or gray markings. The coquí does not have webbed feet. Special toe pads allow it to climb up vertical structures such as tree trunks and to cling to trees and leaves. *Co-kee* is the sound that males make at night to attract females. The *co* sound warns other males away. The *kee* sound attracts females.

FUN FACT
Coquís do not have a tadpole stage. Approximately 17 to 26 days after a female lays eggs, froglets hatch.

HOW TO SPOT

Size: 1 to 2 inches (2.5 to 5 cm) long from snout to vent
Range: Native to Puerto Rico; introduced in US Virgin Islands and Hawaii
Habitat: Forests, gardens, greenhouses, and spaces under rocks and logs
Diet: Spiders, crickets, roaches, and other invertebrates

PUMPKIN TOADLET
(BRACHYCEPHALUS EPHIPPIUM)

Pumpkin toadlets are tiny, poisonous frogs. Their name comes from their warty, bright-yellow or orange skin. The frogs' color warns predators that they are toxic. Their very short limbs put them low to the ground. Pumpkin toadlets have no tadpole stage. After the mother lays the eggs, she rolls them along the ground with her hind feet to cover them. Fully formed frogs hatch approximately 64 days later.

HOW TO SPOT

Size: 0.5 to 0.8 inches (1.3 to 2 cm) long from snout to vent
Range: Atlantic coast of southeastern Brazil
Habitat: Warm and humid mountainous forests
Diet: Primarily springtails, but also insect larvae, mites, and other small invertebrates

FROGS

PURPLE FROG
(NASIKABATRACHUS SAHYADRENSIS)

Purple frogs are also called pignose frogs. This rare frog species is dark purple to grayish in color. They have puffy bodies. Purple frogs eat termites underground. Their hind legs are short. This makes them unable to jump. Instead, they move from place to place by taking long steps. Their front limbs are muscular and have hard palms to help them burrow underground. Purple frogs stay underground most of the year. They come out for a few weeks to mate during monsoon season.

HOW TO SPOT

Size: Up to 2.8 inches (7 cm) long from snout to vent
Range: Western Ghats in India
Habitat: Loose, damp soil close to ponds, ditches, or streams
Diet: Termites

FUN FACT
Purple frog tadpoles have sucker-like mouths. They use these to grip the undersides of rocks until they metamorphose into adults.

RED-EYED TREEFROG
(AGALYCHNIS CALLIDRYAS)

Red-eyed treefrogs are known for their bright-red eyes. Their backs are usually neon green but can be blue or yellow. Red-eyed treefrogs have blue sides with yellow or cream stripes. Their upper legs are also blue. They are great climbers thanks to the large, suction-cup toe pads on their red or bright-orange feet. This allows them to attach to leaves, branches, and sides of trees.

HOW TO SPOT

Size: 1.6 to 2.9 inches (4.1 to 7.4 cm) long from snout to vent

Range: Southern Mexico, Central America, and northern South America

Habitat: Lowland rain forests close to rivers and hills

Diet: Insects and worms

Sleeping red-eyed treefrog

STARTLING PREDATORS

When sleeping, red-eyed treefrogs tuck in their limbs to hide their colorful sides. Gold, webbed eyelids cover their eyes. If they are disturbed, they fling open their eyes. They show predators their large orange feet and bright blue-and-yellow sides. This technique startles predators away.

FROGS

RIOBAMBA MARSUPIAL FROG
(GASTROTHECA RIOBAMBAE)

Riobamba marsupial frogs are also known as Andean marsupial frogs. They get their name from the pouch on the female's back that is used to carry her eggs. Marsupials such as kangaroos also carry their young in pouches. Riobamba marsupial frogs are green and brown. They sometimes have dark spots or stripes on their backs. The underside is cream colored and may also have dark spots. Riobamba marsupial frogs have small heads with large brown eyes, wide mouths, and rounded snouts.

FUN FACT
As a female Riobamba marsupial frog lays her eggs, the male fertilizes them. He pushes them into the female's pouch. When the eggs are ready to hatch, the female uses her back legs to push the tadpoles out of the pouch and into water.

HOW TO SPOT

Size: 1.3 to 2.6 inches (3.4 to 6.6 cm) long from snout to vent

Range: Andes Mountains in Ecuador

Habitat: Pools and streams in mountain fields, farmlands, and rocky hillsides

Diet: Beetles and other invertebrates

SMOKY JUNGLE FROG
(LEPTODACTYLUS PENTADACTYLUS)

Smoky jungle frogs are one of South America's largest frog species. They have reddish-brown or gray skin. They can be solid colored or have dark spots and bars. Males have black spines on the chest and thumbs. During the day, smoky jungle frogs spend most of their time in underground burrows, underneath logs, or in dead leaves. They come out at night to feed. These frogs protect themselves from predators by expanding their bodies to look larger and by releasing a toxin. They also let out a sound like a loud scream when they feel threatened.

HOW TO SPOT

Size: Males up to 7 inches (17.7 cm) long from snout to vent; females up to 7.3 inches (18.5 cm) long

Range: Amazon Basin in Brazil, Bolivia, Peru, Ecuador, Colombia, and French Guiana; also found further north in Costa Rica and Honduras

Habitat: Tropical rain forests near slow-moving streams and swamps

Diet: Other frogs, bird chicks, snakes, and scorpions

FROGS

STRAWBERRY POISON FROG
(OOPHAGA PUMILIO)

Strawberry poison frogs are brightly colored and toxic. They are typically bright red with blue legs, but their backs can be red, blue, white, yellow, green, black, or orange. They sometimes have dark dots on their backs. Their skin is very moist, making it look shiny in bright light. They have small, compact bodies. Their large dark eyes are on the sides of their heads. Strawberry poison frogs spend most of their time on the rain forest floor in fallen leaves. But they also climb trees and vines.

HOW TO SPOT

Size: 0.7 to 0.9 inches (1.7 to 2.4 cm) long from snout to vent
Range: Central America
Habitat: Rain forests and cacao and banana groves
Diet: Small insects and invertebrates such as mites

FUN FACT
Female strawberry poison frogs carry their tadpoles to small pools of water in bromeliad plants. The mother lays unfertilized eggs for the tadpoles to eat until they become adults.

SUMACO HORNED TREEFROG
(HEMIPHRACTUS PROBOSCIDEUS)

The Sumaco horned treefrog has a large head with a pointed snout. These frogs have large eyes with small points above them and jagged growths out of the skull. Fang-like growths on their lower jaws look like teeth. Sumaco horned treefrogs are usually shades of brown with dark streaks on their faces and dark bands on their legs. The underside is brown with orange or light-brown spots.

HOW TO SPOT

Size: 1.7 to 2.6 inches (4.3 to 6.6 cm) long from snout to vent
Range: Colombia, Ecuador, and Peru
Habitat: Humid forests in lowlands or mountains
Diet: Large invertebrates, small lizards, and other frogs

FUN FACT
When threatened, Sumaco horned treefrogs will show predators their bright-yellow mouth and tongue to scare them away.

FROGS

SURINAM HORNED FROG
(CERATOPHRYS CORNUTA)

Surinam horned frogs can be tan, lime green, or dark green. Sometimes they are a mix of all three colors. Surinam horned frogs have white mouths and gray undersides. Their most identifiable feature is the fleshy horns above the eyes. The frog's coloring and horns help it blend into its environment. The horns may be confused for leaves. Surinam horned frogs bury themselves in leaves with only their heads sticking out. They wait for prey to appear, and then they strike. Surinam horned frogs will eat almost anything that fits in their mouths.

HOW TO SPOT

Size: 2.8 to 5.9 inches (7 to 15 cm) long from snout to vent

Range: Amazon River running through Colombia, Ecuador, the Guianas, Venezuela, Peru, Bolivia, and Brazil

Habitat: Open areas within forests, leaves on the forest floor, and near freshwater marshes and pools in the forest area

Diet: Small mammals, fish, amphibians, and reptiles

FUN FACT

Surinam horned frogs are often called Pac-Man frogs. This is because their extremely wide mouths resemble the video game character.

SURINAM TOAD *(PIPA PIPA)*

Surinam toads have flat, square bodies. Their heads are triangular, and their nostrils rest at the ends of two narrow tubes on their snouts. Their skin is rough. It is spotted with brown, tan, or olive colorings. Each finger on their front limbs has a star-shaped tip, giving it the nickname "star-fingered toad." They are camouflaged to live life in muddy river bottoms. They blend in with the leaves and rocks. They have small black eyes and hind feet like flippers. They use their front fingers to find food and put it in their mouths.

HOW TO SPOT

Size: 4 to 8 inches (10.1 to 20.3 cm) long from snout to vent
Range: Eastern South America and Trinidad
Habitat: Muddy ponds and swamps
Diet: Worms, insects, crustaceans, and small fish

MATING SURINAM TOADS

Surinam toads have an interesting mating ritual. A male and female swim to the surface of the water, holding tightly together and spinning in circles. The female lays eggs, the male fertilizes them, and the eggs stick to the female's back. The eggs sink into the skin. They develop there until fully developed frogs hatch.

FROGS

TITICACA WATER FROG
(TELMATOBIUS CULEUS)

Titicaca water frogs are the largest known fully aquatic frog species in the world. They live their entire lives underwater and only come up to the surface when their oxygen is low. They have extra skin folds on their bodies that make them look baggy. To get oxygen from the water, they make a movement like a push-up. This pushes more water across their skin folds and provides more surface area to breathe through their skin. They have flattened heads, rounded faces, and large, forward-pointing eyes with round black pupils. Their backs are black, olive green, or dark green. Their undersides are pearl or white. Their back feet are fully webbed.

HOW TO SPOT

Size: 2.9 to 5.4 inches (7.4 to 13.8 cm) long from snout to vent
Range: Lake Titicaca in Peru and Bolivia
Habitat: Underwater in muddy, sandy areas near rocks or vegetation
Diet: Crustaceans, insects, snails, fish, and worms

TURTLE FROG (MYOBATRACHUS GOULDII)

Turtle frogs look like turtles missing their shells. The turtle frog is a small frog that can be grayish brown, yellowish brown, or pink. It sometimes has dark patches on its back. The underside is solid white or white with dark patches. Turtle frogs' heads are small with tiny eyes. They have claws and short, muscular arms and legs. Unlike other burrowing frogs, turtle frogs use their front claws to go headfirst into the sand instead of using their hind legs to burrow backward. They will keep digging until they are at least 3 feet (0.9 m) underground.

FUN FACT
Turtle frogs do not undergo metamorphosis. They come straight out of the egg as baby frogs.

HOW TO SPOT
Size: 2 inches (5 cm) long from snout to vent
Range: Western Australia
Habitat: Sandy soil
Diet: Termites

FROGS

TUSKED FROG *(ADELOTUS BREVIS)*

Tusked frogs get their name from their two large lower teeth, or tusks. Both males and females have the tusks, but they are larger in males. Males use them for fighting or defending their territory. The tusks do not show when the frogs' mouths are closed. Tusked frogs are olive green or black. They often have dark spots on their backs. Their undersides are spotted black and white. Their legs have orange or red spots.

HOW TO SPOT

Size: 1.6 to 2 inches (4 to 5 cm) long from snout to vent
Range: Eastern Australia
Habitat: Forests and grasslands, often near water
Diet: Snails, insects, and other invertebrates

FUN FACT

Unlike many frog species, male tusked frogs are larger than females.

VIETNAMESE MOSSY FROG
(THELODERMA CORTICALE)

Vietnamese mossy frogs have rough, uneven skin with spines and bumpy growths. They are shades of green with red, brownish-black, or black patches. The coloring makes the frog look like a clump of moss. When resting, Vietnamese mossy frogs flatten out and look as wide as they are long. This allows them to disappear into moss-covered rocks. They have sticky toe pads that allow them to cling to rocky surfaces. They are active at night and spend most of the day hiding under rocks. The Vietnamese mossy frog can curl into a tight ball when threatened.

HOW TO SPOT

Size: 2.5 to 3.5 inches (6.4 to 8.9 cm) long from snout to vent

Range: Northern Vietnam

Habitat: Flooded caves and banks of rocky mountain streams

Diet: Large insects such as crickets and cockroaches

FROGS

WALLACE'S FLYING FROG
(RHACOPHORUS NIGROPALMATUS)

Wallace's flying frogs do not actually fly. They can glide from tall trees. For this reason, they are also called parachute frogs. They are some of the largest flying frogs. Wallace's flying frogs have black webbing between their toes. When threatened, they spread their toes and leap from trees, gliding on the air. Their hind legs are longer than their front legs. This allows them to get more force when they push off to glide. Toe pads help them grip trees after landing. Wallace's flying frogs have flat heads and large eyes. Their backs are green, and their sides, inner thighs, and undersides are yellow.

FUN FACT
Wallace's flying frogs spend most of their lives in trees. They come down only to mate and lay eggs.

HOW TO SPOT

Size: 3.5 to 3.9 inches (9 to 10 cm) long from snout to vent
Range: Malaysia and Borneo
Habitat: Tropical forests
Diet: Insects and other small invertebrates

WESTERN GREEN AND GOLDEN BELL FROG *(LITORIA MOOREI)*

Western green and golden bell frogs are large, powerful frogs with long back limbs. They have a wide range of possible colors. After lying in the sun, the frogs' backs can be green with gold spots. In colder conditions, they are often darker brown. Their undersides are pale green to light brown. Their toes are partially webbed, and the tips of their fingers and toes have toe pads. These frogs are often called motorbike frogs. This is because the first part of their call sounds like a motorcycle changing gears.

HOW TO SPOT

Size: Up to 3 inches (7.5 cm) long from snout to vent
Range: Southwestern Australia near Perth
Habitat: Swamps, lakes, streams, dams, and ponds
Diet: Invertebrates and smaller frogs

FUN FACT
Western green and golden bell frogs can climb low tree branches or shrubs, rocks, brick walls, and even windows as high as 6.6 feet (2 m).

FROGS

WOOD FROG *(LITHOBATES SYLVATICUS)*

Wood frogs are different shades of brown, red, green, or gray. The underside is white, sometimes with dark spots. Females are usually more brightly colored than males. Wood frogs are found farther north than any other amphibian in North America. They survive the cold winter by creating a special substance that fills their cells and keeps them from freezing to death. Up to 70 percent of their body freezes. While wood frogs are frozen, their hearts stop beating and they stop breathing. When the weather warms up, the frogs thaw out and come back to life.

HOW TO SPOT

Size: 1.4 to 3 inches (3.5 to 7.6 cm) long from snout to vent
Range: From northern Georgia to the northeastern United States, through Canada and into Alaska
Habitat: Tundra, thickets, wet meadows, bogs, and forests
Diet: Land insects, arachnids, moth larvae, slugs, and snails

REGULATING HEAT

Wood frogs can change color from dark to light very quickly, which helps them control their body temperature. They get darker when it's cold in order to trap heat. They get lighter when it's warm to keep from getting too hot.

YELLOW-BELLIED TOAD
(BOMBINA VARIEGATA)

Yellow-bellied toads have bright-yellow or yellow-orange undersides with black markings. The frogs' backs are dark gray to olive green with small, pointy warts that look like spines. The tips of their toes are yellow or orange. When the weather cools, they leave the water and hibernate in underground burrows.

HOW TO SPOT

Size: 1 to 2 inches (2.5 to 5.1 cm) long from snout to vent

Range: Central and southern Europe

Habitat: Ponds, lakes, fast-moving streams and rivers, and pools of water in forests, grasslands, and meadows

Diet: Land and water invertebrates

FUN FACT
Yellow-bellied toads will live in almost any type of water available. This includes puddles, ditches, and wheel ruts filled with water.

TOADS

AMERICAN TOAD
(ANAXYRUS AMERICANUS)

American toads are also called hop toads. This is because their short legs limit them to hopping or walking rather than jumping. They have round bodies with thick, dry, warty skin. Their backs are usually brown, reddish, or olive with dark marks. Depending on humidity, temperature, and stress levels, they can appear lighter or darker. American toads have poison glands behind their eyes. These release a toxin that will irritate the eyes and mouths of most predators. The toxin can also cause paralysis or death.

HOW TO SPOT

Size: 2 to 4 inches (5 to 10.2 cm) long from snout to vent
Range: Eastern Canada and the United States
Habitat: Anywhere with fresh water and heavy plant cover; common in forests, gardens, and fields
Diet: Small insects such as beetles, moths, and earthworms

BLOWING UP

When American toads sense danger, they have several strategies for survival. Most of the time they will stay still, counting on camouflage to keep them hidden. Sometimes an American toad will blow up its body like a balloon and stretch its back legs to look larger. This is especially common when threatened by snakes.

ASIATIC TOAD *(BUFO GARGARIZANS)*

Asiatic toads have bumpy skin with a distinctive ridge down each side of the back. They are usually dark gray, olive gray, or olive brown. Their undersides are yellowish or grayish. They have black bands along their sides. The bands stretch from the glands behind the neck to the underside. Asiatic toads hibernate on land or in deep rivers and lakes. Hibernation begins in the fall and can last until April or May.

HOW TO SPOT

Size: 2.2 to 4 inches (5.6 to 10.2 cm) long from snout to vent
Range: Japan, Korea, China, and Russia
Habitat: Forests, grasslands, and meadows
Diet: Insects

FUN FACT
Asiatic toads are commonly used in traditional Chinese medicine. The toads' venom and skin can be used to treat pain, inflammation, and certain cancers.

TOADS

CANE TOAD *(RHINELLA MARINA)*

Cane toads are large toads with rough, dry skin that is covered in warts. Their color can be gray, olive, yellow brown, or red brown. Their undersides are lighter with brown spots. The toad's bony head has a pointed snout and ridges over the eyes. Humans introduced cane toads to Australia in 1935. Beetles were eating the sugarcane crop. People hoped the toads would control the beetle population. Instead, cane toads became one of the most invasive species in the world. Most Australian predators have no immunity to cane toad venom. Cane toads often kill predators that try to eat them.

HOW TO SPOT

Size: 5.9 to 9.4 inches (15 to 23.8 cm) long from snout to vent

Range: Native to southern Texas, Central America, and South America; introduced in Australia, the Caribbean, Florida, and Hawaii

Habitat: Sand dunes, coastal grasslands, edges of rain forests, and near mangrove trees

Diet: Insects, snails, and food left out for pets

FUN FACT
Cane toads aren't good climbers, and they can't jump high. They move in short, quick hops rather than leaping.

GOLDEN TOAD *(INCILIUS PERIGLENES)*

Golden toads are known by several different names. The most common are Monteverde golden toads or Monteverde toads. The species was found only in the Monteverde Cloud Forest Preserve in Costa Rica. The males and females of this species had different characteristics. Males were orange, while females were black with red spots outlined in yellow. These differences emerged in adulthood. They lived underground most of the year and came out between April and June to breed. The golden toad was last spotted in the wild in 1989. Many scientists believe that it's extinct.

Male

HOW TO SPOT

Size: 1.5 to 2.2 inches (3.9 to 5.6 cm) long from snout to vent

Range: Monteverde Cloud Forest Preserve in Costa Rica

Habitat: Wet, mountainous forests

Diet: Small invertebrates

GOING, GOING, GONE

In 1987, the golden toad population dropped substantially. Scientists believed that unstable weather caused their breeding pools to dry up before the larvae developed. They now believe a disease was the main reason for this species' decline. Conservationists and scientists hope that the toads are just hiding until the conditions are right to reproduce. The toads' breeding area is protected in case they come back.

TOADS

GUTTURAL TOAD
(SCLEROPHRYS GUTTURALIS)

Guttural toads are a common toad species that are named for their loud calls. Their backs are light brownish yellow with dark-brown markings. There is often a pale stripe down the spine. Guttural toads have pairs of brown spots between the eyes and bulging glands behind the eyes. Their undersides are rough, and they have slightly webbed toes. Guttural toads live mostly on land, but they can be found in bodies of water such as ponds. They hunt for food at night and shelter during the day in shady spots and under rocks and logs.

HOW TO SPOT

Size: 2.4 to 4.7 inches (6.2 to 12 cm) long from snout to vent
Range: Central and southern Africa
Habitat: Woodlands, savannas, grasslands, and garden ponds
Diet: Lizards, insects, and other frogs

Male

FUN FACT
Guttural toads are invasive in parts of South Africa. They threaten the survival of native frog and toad species because they compete for habitat, food, and breeding areas.

MONGOLIAN TOAD
(STRAUCHBUFO RADDEI)

Mongolian toads have light-olive, greenish-gray, or gray backs with large dark spots. There is a narrow stripe down the back, sometimes with red dots. Mongolian toads' undersides are light gray with a few dark spots. Mongolian toads are active on warm, sunny days. They hibernate from September or October to April or May. They often hibernate in groups. Hibernation usually takes place on land, but in northern regions, they spend the winter in holes between 3.3 and 6.6 feet (1 to 2 m) deep.

HOW TO SPOT

Size: 1.6 to 3.5 inches (4 to 8.9 cm) long from snout to vent
Range: China, Mongolia, North Korea, and Russia
Habitat: Edges of forests, meadows, and grasslands, and in areas with sandy, rocky, or loose clay or gravel
Diet: Spiders, caterpillars, beetles, and ants

TOADS

NATTERJACK TOAD
(EPIDALEA CALAMITA)

Natterjack toads have flat bodies with partially webbed feet. The skin on their backs is warty and olive green with a yellow stripe down the middle. They have numerous warts on the sides of their backs with dark-brown, red, or green coloring. Males have off-white throats that may have smudges of purple or blue. The underside is creamy white with dark green spots, and the eyes are golden or green.

HOW TO SPOT

Size: 2.4 to 3.1 inches (6 to 8 cm) long from snout to vent

Range: Southwestern and central Europe, into the British Isles and western Russia

Habitat: Coastal areas near shallow pools, sand dunes, moors, and marshes

Diet: Small reptiles and small invertebrates such as worms, ants, mollusks, woodlice, spiders, moths, and ground beetles

FUN FACT

Natterjack toads are one of the rarest toad species in the United Kingdom. This is due to factors such as water pollution, loss of habitat, and drought. Now they are part of a conservation effort, protected by law in the United Kingdom and European Union.

Male

PANAMANIAN GOLDEN FROG
(ATELOPUS ZETEKI)

Panamanian golden frogs are small toads with brightly colored bodies. Although they are called frogs, they are actually categorized as true toads. Their heads are long with pointed snouts. Their bodies are slim with long legs. Their backs are smooth and yellow with black spots. Glands on their skin produce a toxin that comes from the insects they eat. Males attract females by waving their arms and legs, twitching their heads, hopping in place, and stomping the ground. They are critically endangered and possibly extinct in the wild.

HOW TO SPOT

Size: 1.4 to 2.5 inches (3.5 to 6.3 cm) long from snout to vent
Range: Panama
Habitat: Rain forests, mountain forests, and streams in wet and dry forests
Diet: Insects and other small invertebrates

FUN FACT
Panamanian golden frogs are a cultural symbol in Panama. They appear in artwork and legends, and they are considered good luck.

TOADS

RED-SPOTTED TOAD
(ANAXYRUS PUNCTATUS)

Red-spotted toads are small with dry, warty skin. Glands on the sides of the head release poison. This poison defends against predators. Red-spotted toads are olive, brown, or light gray with orange or red warts. They are good climbers and can easily scale rocks. They move slowly, crawling or walking with short hops. These toads are nocturnal and stay underground or underneath objects during the day. Males produce a shrill, high-pitched, ten-second musical call at night.

HOW TO SPOT

Size: Up to 3 inches (7.6 cm) long from snout to vent
Range: Southwestern United States
Habitat: Rocky areas where they can use the cracks in the rocks for shelter
Diet: Insects such as ants, bees, and beetles; sometimes smaller amphibians

FUN FACT
Red-spotted toads survive well in dry environments. They can survive losing 40 percent of their body water.

SAMBAS STREAM TOAD
(ANSONIA LATIDISCA)

Sambas stream toads are commonly called Bornean rainbow toads. This is for their bright colors and the place where they were first discovered. Their rough backs have red, green, yellow, and purple spots similar to warts. Their coloring warns predators that they are poisonous. Sambas stream toads have long, skinny legs. They live entirely in trees but might reproduce in streams. The toad's coloring has been compared to moss. Scientists believe this is an adaptation that allows the toads to camouflage on the moss-covered tree bark where they live.

HOW TO SPOT

Size: 1.2 to 2 inches (3 to 5.1 cm) long from snout to vent
Range: Island of Borneo in Indonesia and Malaysia
Habitat: Forests and wetlands
Diet: Small insects found in the rain forest

EXCITING DISCOVERY

Explorers rediscovered the Sambas stream toad in 2011. This was 87 years after it had last been seen in the wild. Researchers found it as part of a global search for lost amphibians. Prior to 2011, scientists had only ever seen drawings of the species, never a photograph.

TOADS

SOUTHEAST ASIAN TOAD
(DUTTAPHRYNUS MELANOSTICTUS)

Southeast Asian toads are one of the most common toads in Southeast Asia. They are medium-large with small heads and short hind limbs. Their color ranges from gray to reddish brown. The most common color is pale yellow brown with dark or reddish-brown spots. The toads' backs are covered in spiny warts with black or dark spots. Their heads have black, bony ridges above their eyes. Southeast Asian toads are poor climbers and can't jump very high.

HOW TO SPOT

Size: 2.2 to 3.3 inches (5.7 to 8.3 cm) long from snout to vent
Range: South and Southeast Asia and southern China
Habitat: Tropical and subtropical forests
Diet: Insects

FUN FACT
Southeast Asian toads are invasive in Madagascar. Scientists believe they accidentally arrived there in shipping containers.

STARRY NIGHT HARLEQUIN TOAD *(ATELOPUS ARSYECUE)*

Starry night harlequin toads are a critically endangered species. In 2019, scientists rediscovered them after not having seen them since 1991. Starry night harlequin toads are shiny black with white spots. Their name comes from the clear, starry night skies in their habitat. They have slim bodies and pointy snouts. Their toes are pointed. Most harlequin toads are endangered. Conservationists are working to protect them and their habitats.

HOW TO SPOT

Size: Under 2 inches (5.1 cm) long from snout to vent
Range: Sierra Nevada de Santa Marta mountain range in Colombia
Habitat: Forests, wetlands, and grasslands
Diet: Invertebrates

SACRED TOADS

The Arhuaco people of Colombia have a special relationship with the starry night harlequin toad. The people consider the toads, called *gouna*, to be sacred. The people rely on the toads' singing to indicate when to plant crops. The Arhuaco people worked closely with conservationists to allow scientists to study starry night toads in a way that respected their habitat and Arhuaco culture.

TOADS

WESTERN LEOPARD TOAD
(SCLEROPHRYS PANTHERINA)

Western leopard toads are larger than any other toads in their geographic range. They have rough, dry skin with leopard-like brown spots on their bright-yellow backs. The toad has two red or brown glands behind its eyes and a cream line down the middle of its back. During the summer months, western leopard toads are inactive during the day and come out at night to hunt for food. This is when they build up their food supplies to prepare for breeding season. Western leopard toads are often called snoring frogs because of the male's mating call.

FUN FACT
The biggest threat to western leopard toads comes from cars. The toads often have to cross roads to get to and from the water where they breed.

HOW TO SPOT

Size: 5.5 inches (14 cm) long from snout to vent
Range: Western Cape of South Africa
Habitat: Natural vegetation, farms, and fertilizer heaps in gardens
Diet: Snails, beetles, bugs, earthworms, and caterpillars

WESTERN TOAD *(ANAXYRUS BOREAS)*

Western toads have thick bodies, short legs, and rough, bumpy skin. Their backs are usually brownish gray or brownish green. But they can be nearly black, green, or reddish brown. There is a white or cream-colored stripe on the spine. Western toads have reddish-brown glands behind their eyes. They use the toxins in those glands to defend against predators. Western toads are nocturnal when found in low altitudes and active during the day at higher altitudes. During the winter, they hibernate underground.

HOW TO SPOT

Size: 2.2 to 5.7 inches (5.5 to 14.5 cm) long from snout to vent

Range: Western United States and western Canada

Habitat: Aquatic habitats ranging from ditches to lakes

Diet: Insects, spiders, slugs, and worms

SALAMANDERS

ALPINE SALAMANDER
(SALAMANDRA ATRA)

Alpine salamanders have smooth, shiny, brown or black bodies. They have slightly stretched heads and kidney-shaped glands in front of each ear. They have a double row of poison glands running down their backs. Another row of poison glands runs down either side of the body to the tail. Alpine salamanders live entirely on land and are very active at night or after rainfall. During the day, they hide in rock openings or burrows. Alpine salamanders hibernate between six and eight months depending on their altitude.

HOW TO SPOT

Size: Males up to 5.7 inches (14.4 cm) long; females up to 5.9 inches (15.1 cm) long
Range: Swiss Alps; some populations in Dinaric Alps
Habitat: Alpine meadows, woodlands, and forests
Diet: Invertebrates

FUN FACT
Developing Alpine salamanders feed on their mother's eggs. It takes two to three years for Alpine salamanders to develop before they are born live.

AXOLOTL *(AMBYSTOMA MEXICANUM)*

Axolotl means "water dog" in the Nahuatl language of the Aztecs. It refers to the Aztec god Xolotl, a god of fire and lightning. Axolotls are dark with greenish spots. They have wide, flat bodies with large heads and feather-like gills. They use their gills to breathe underwater and occasionally come up for air. Their mouths look like they're grinning. They can lighten or darken their skin as needed for camouflage. In the wild, axolotls are native to only two lakes in Mexico. Lake Chalco no longer exists, and Lake Xochimilco is mostly swamps and canals. As a result, axolotls are considered critically endangered.

HOW TO SPOT

Size: 6 to 18 inches (15.2 to 45.7 cm) long
Range: Lake Xochimilco in Mexico City
Habitat: Lakes
Diet: Worms, mollusks, crustaceans, insect larvae, and small fish

FUN FACT

Axolotls are known for their regenerative abilities. Like some other salamanders, they can regrow almost any part of themselves, including parts of their brains and entire limbs.

Albino axolotl

SALAMANDERS

CALIFORNIA GIANT SALAMANDER *(DICAMPTODON ENSATUS)*

California giant salamanders have patterns of dark spots on light-brown, brass-colored backs. Their long tails are flattened for swimming. They have four toes on their front feet and five on their back feet, which are adapted for digging and climbing. They dig to find food and to create protective cover. California giant salamanders are nocturnal. They stay out of direct sunlight. They need damp surroundings to keep their skin from drying out.

HOW TO SPOT

Size: 6.7 to 12 inches (17 to 30.5 cm) long
Range: West Coast of North America
Habitat: Lakes, ponds, rivers, and streams
Diet: Land snails and slugs; insects such as beetles, caddisfly larvae, moths, and flies; small mammals such as shrews and white-footed mice; and other amphibians

FIGHTERS

California giant salamanders are extremely aggressive. They will bite, beat their tails, and make themselves look intimidating to scare predators away. They will also use the glands on the tops of their tails to release bad-tasting chemicals.

CHINESE GIANT SALAMANDER
(ANDRIAS DAVIDIANUS)

The Chinese giant salamander is the world's largest amphibian. It lives underwater, but it doesn't have gills. The salamander absorbs oxygen through its skin, using folds of skin along its sides to increase exposure to oxygen. This helps the salamander breathe. Chinese giant salamanders can be various colors, such as gray, brown, or greenish. They also have dark markings on their skin. These salamanders have short heads with small eyes behind their nostrils. They find prey by sensing vibrations in the water through sensory knots along the sides of their bodies. Chinese giant salamanders are nicknamed "baby fish" because they make a sound like a baby crying.

HOW TO SPOT

Size: Up to 5.9 feet (1.8 m) long
Range: China
Habitat: Mountain rivers and large streams with rocky bottoms
Diet: Fish, frogs, worms, snails, insects, crayfish, crabs, and smaller salamanders

FUN FACT
The Chinese giant salamander's relatives can be traced back to amphibians who lived during the Jurassic Period approximately 170 million years ago.

SALAMANDERS

COMMON MUDPUPPY
(NECTURUS MACULOSUS)

Common mudpuppies are rarely seen because they stay under rocks, logs, or weeds during the day. Their bodies are rusty brown, reddish gray, or black, and their undersides are gray or white. Their bodies are flat with smooth, slippery skin. They have flat heads, wide tails, short legs, and feathery gills. Common mudpuppies keep their limbs tight against their bodies and use their tails to push themselves through water. They rely on their sense of smell to find food.

HOW TO SPOT

Size: 7.9 to 13 inches (20 to 33 cm) long

Range: Southeast Manitoba to southern Quebec in Canada, and the Great Lakes Basin to Louisiana in the United States

Habitat: Weedy ponds, large lakes, rivers, and streams

Diet: Worms, fish eggs, aquatic insects, crayfish, and small fish

COMMON WORM SALAMANDER
(OEDIPINA UNIFORMIS)

Common worm salamanders have very slim, long bodies and tiny limbs. This makes them look like worms. Their backs can be tan, dark brown, gray, or black. Their undersides are lighter gray black. Their heads, bodies, and tails are the same width, and their tiny hands and feet are almost always webbed. Their tails can be up to twice the length of their bodies. Common worm salamanders are nocturnal and shy. They hide under fallen leaves, wet mosses, and decaying logs during the day.

HOW TO SPOT

Size: Up to 8.5 inches (21.5 cm) long
Range: Costa Rica
Habitat: Humid mountain forests
Diet: Small invertebrates

FUN FACT
When a common worm salamander is caught by a predator, it forcefully whips its tail back and forth to escape. It can even break off its tail.

SALAMANDERS

CORSICAN FIRE SALAMANDER
(SALAMANDRA CORSICA)

Corsican fire salamanders have smooth, shiny black bodies with yellow spots on their backs and feet. Their heads are round and wide. They have bright-yellow glands behind each ear and two lines of poison glands running parallel down their sides. Two uneven rows of glands also run down their tails. Corsican fire salamanders bask on large boulders covered in fallen leaves and mosses. They cool off underneath the boulders in the moist shade.

HOW TO SPOT

Size: 4.7 to 11.8 inches (12 to 30 cm) long
Range: Corsica
Habitat: Forests near freshwater streams or shaded ponds
Diet: Insects, arachnids, terrestrial mollusks, centipedes, and earthworms

FUN FACT
Some Corsican fire salamanders undergo metamorphosis. Others give birth to fully developed young.

DWARF SALAMANDER
(EURYCEA QUADRIDIGITATA)

Dwarf salamanders are one of the smallest vertebrates found in North America. They are light bronze, brownish yellow, or black. They have black or brown lines on their sides from their eyes to their tails. Their undersides have brown dots. Their tails are flattened. Approximately 60 percent of the salamander's body length comes from its tail. When dwarf salamanders hatch, they come out of the egg with small external gills. The larvae spend several months in the water before turning into adults.

HOW TO SPOT

Size: Up to 3.5 inches (8.9 cm) long
Range: Eastern and southern US coastal plains
Habitat: Around swamps and at the edges of ponds in pine forests or savannas
Diet: Small invertebrates

SALAMANDERS

EASTERN RED-BACKED SALAMANDER *(PLETHODON CINEREUS)*

Eastern red-backed salamanders have two genetic variations in their skin color. In the red-back variation, a wide stripe runs down the salamander's back from head to tail. The stripe is usually red or brownish orange but can be pink, yellow, or gray. In the lead-back variation, the salamander is solid black or gray with black and white spots on its belly and lower sides. Eastern red-backed salamanders do not have lungs. They breathe through their skin and the lining in their mouths and throats. They need moisture to breathe and therefore have to live in damp environments.

Lead-back variation

HOW TO SPOT

Size: 2 to 5 inches (5.1 to 12.7 cm) long
Range: Eastern United States and Canada
Habitat: Woodlands, ravines, and river valleys
Diet: Small invertebrates such as arachnids, worms, and insects

Red-back variation

FUN FACT

An eastern red-backed salamander marks its space with its scent and feces. This provides other salamanders with important information about the eastern red-backed salamander's territory, size, and identity.

FIRE SALAMANDER
(SALAMANDRA SALAMANDRA)

Fire salamanders are black with yellow spots or stripes. Their undersides are dark gray with spots. Their bodies are usually longer than their tails, and they have thick limbs. Fire salamanders have large glands behind their eyes and rows of poison glands down the length of their bodies. These salamanders are mostly active on mild nights and are inactive in extreme temperatures. They spend most of their time hiding underneath rocks and logs to stay moist. These concealed spots also protect them from predators.

HOW TO SPOT

Size: 5.9 to 9.8 inches (15 to 25 cm) long

Range: Central and southern Europe, into northern Africa and the Middle East

Habitat: Woodlands with shade, ponds, and streams for breeding

Diet: Small invertebrates such as insects, earthworms, and slugs

OUT OF THE FLAMES

The word *salamander* comes from an old Arabic term meaning "lives in fire." According to folklore, fire salamanders were fireproof. Salamanders would crawl out from logs thrown on fires. Their skin is not actually fireproof. But the name stuck.

SALAMANDERS

GEORGIA BLIND SALAMANDER
(EURYCEA WALLACEI)

Georgia blind salamanders have white, slightly transparent bodies with a hint of yellow or pink. They have red gills, four skinny legs, and long, flat heads. The eyes are very small and undeveloped. This is an adaptation to their completely dark environment. They mostly stay on the bottoms of pools in underground caves. They have been spotted underwater, moving over flat surfaces and ledges.

HOW TO SPOT

Size: 1 to 2 inches (2.5 to 5 cm) long
Range: Georgia into Florida in the United States
Habitat: Underground pools and streams in caves and sinkholes
Diet: Small aquatic invertebrates such as seed shrimp

FUN FACT
Georgia blind salamanders are defined as aquatic troglobites. This means that they are adapted for life in underground aquatic environments, such as caves.

GOLD-STRIPED SALAMANDER
(CHIOGLOSSA LUSITANICA)

Gold-striped salamanders have long, slim bodies with long tails. The tail makes up 67 percent of the total body length. Gold-striped salamanders have dark-brown bodies with two golden-brown stripes on their backs. They have long, narrow heads, large eyes, and long, sticky tongues. Their front legs have four toes and are smaller and skinnier than their back legs. Their back legs have five toes. In the summer, gold-striped salamanders enter a sleep state, but rainfall can fuel activity. They usually hibernate in the winter and are active in spring and fall, when they feed and reproduce.

Gold-striped salamander with its eggs

HOW TO SPOT

Size: Up to 6 inches (15.2 cm) long
Range: Northwestern Spain and north-central Portugal
Habitat: Wet, mountainous areas
Diet: Flies and other insects

SALAMANDERS

HELLBENDER
(CRYPTOBRANCHUS ALLEGANIENSIS)

The hellbender is the largest aquatic salamander in the United States. Hellbenders have long, thick bodies, flat heads, and wrinkled sides. Their tails are shaped like paddles. Their skin is brownish gray with black spots on the back. Adult hellbenders have lungs, but they don't rely on them for breathing. They mostly breathe through their skin. The wrinkled skin folds on their bodies and legs increase the area of skin available for absorbing oxygen. Hellbenders hardly ever swim. Instead, they move by crawling along river bottoms, using their rough toe pads to grip.

HOW TO SPOT

Size: 1 to 2.3 feet (0.3 to 0.7 m) long
Range: Appalachian region and the Midwestern United States
Habitat: Under large rocks or boulders buried in cold, fast-flowing streams
Diet: Crayfish, small fish, and worms

FUN FACT
The scientific name *Cryptobranchus* is Latin for "hidden gills." Hellbenders got this name because they lose their gills around 18 months and absorb them into their bodies.

JAPANESE CLAWED SALAMANDER
(ONYCHODACTYLUS JAPONICUS)

Japanese clawed salamanders are lungless salamanders. They have thin brown bodies with an orange stripe down the center of their backs. They have orange spots on the backs of their heads and on their legs. Their tails are long and slightly flattened at the end. Japanese clawed salamanders have structures on their toes that are like claws. They live mainly on land, but they stay close to water. They are often found under wet rocks or logs beside streams.

HOW TO SPOT

Size: 4 to 7 inches (10.2 to 17.8 cm) long
Range: Honshu and Shikoku Islands, Japan
Habitat: Wetlands and forests
Diet: Aquatic invertebrates; adults also eat land invertebrates

SALAMANDERS

JAPANESE GIANT SALAMANDER *(ANDRIAS JAPONICUS)*

Japanese giant salamanders rarely come on land unless they are looking for a new habitat. They are the second-largest salamander species in the world. They have spotted brown, bumpy, thick, wrinkly skin. Their heads are large and round. They have small eyes and poor eyesight. The Japanese giant salamander has one lung, which it uses to help float in the water. But these salamanders breathe through their skin. When threatened, Japanese giant salamanders release a toxic substance that smells like peppers. This has given them the nickname "big pepper fish" in Japan.

HOW TO SPOT

Size: Up to 4.9 feet (1.5 m) long
Range: Northern region of Kyushu Island and western Honshu Island, Japan
Habitat: Cold, fast-moving mountain streams
Diet: Invertebrates, fish, and smaller amphibians

FUN FACT

Male salamanders are often called "den masters." The female leaves the den after laying her eggs, and the male is in charge of protecting the eggs until they are ready to hatch.

MARBLED SALAMANDER
(AMBYSTOMA OPACUM)

Marbled salamanders are sometimes called banded salamanders because of the white or light-gray bands across their heads, backs, and tails. Males are slightly smaller and have silvery-white bands, which become white during breeding season. Females have silvery-gray bands. Marbled salamanders are solitary and spend most of the day under fallen leaves or up to 3 feet (0.9 m) underground. They usually come into contact with each other only during breeding season. Marbled salamanders breed on land in the fall.

HOW TO SPOT

Size: 3.5 to 4.2 inches (9 to 10.7 cm) long
Range: Eastern United States
Habitat: Damp woodlands close to ponds or streams
Diet: Small worms, insects, slugs, and snails

FUN FACT
In the fall, female marbled salamanders lay their eggs under logs. They stay with the eggs to keep them moist. The eggs hatch once it rains. If it doesn't rain all season, the eggs will hatch in the spring.

SALAMANDERS

NAUTA MUSHROOM-TONGUE SALAMANDER
(BOLITOGLOSSA ALTAMAZONICA)

Nauta mushroom-tongue salamanders are small, lungless salamanders. They have wide heads, short limbs, and long tails. Their hands and feet are webbed. They vary in color but often have solid dark-brown backs. Their undersides are spotted and lighter than their backs and sides. They are nocturnal and stay close to the ground during the day, hiding in fallen leaves, bark from logs, and abandoned termite nests.

HOW TO SPOT

Size: 1.9 to 2.3 inches (4.7 to 5.8 cm) long from snout to vent
Range: Central and South America
Habitat: Lowland rain forests
Diet: Ants, beetles, and grasshoppers

OLM *(PROTEUS ANGUINUS)*

Olms are a species of blind salamander. They have long, slim bodies. Their eyes are very small and covered by skin. These eyes can only sense darkness and light. Olms have large, feathery, pink gills on either side of their heads. Their tails are flattened, and small fins run along the top and bottom. Their skin is usually creamy white, but it can have a pinkish tint. Their undersides are semitransparent and the outlines of their organs are visible. Olms can go months or years without needing food.

> **FUN FACT**
> An olm's skin will turn dark violet to black when it's exposed to light. It will go back to white when the olm is back in darkness.

HOW TO SPOT

Size: 9.1 to 9.8 inches (23 to 25 cm) long

Range: Italy, Slovenia, Croatia, and Bosnia and Herzegovina; possibly into Montenegro and Serbia

Habitat: Underground freshwater lakes and streams in limestone caves

Diet: Mostly insects, but they will eat anything they can catch and fit in their mouths

SALAMANDERS

RETICULATED SIREN
(SIREN RETICULATA)

Reticulated sirens are a rare species of salamander. The species was first detected in the United States in 2018. This was the first new siren species to be identified since 1944. Reticulated sirens are large, completely aquatic, eel-like salamanders with large external gills, leopard-like spots, and no hind limbs. Their backs are greenish yellow with greenish-purple spots. They are able to live on land, but they spend most of their time in water.

HOW TO SPOT

Size: 2 feet (0.6 m) long or longer
Range: Southern Alabama and northwestern Florida
Habitat: Bottom of creeks and swamps in pine forests
Diet: Crustaceans, small insects, and sometimes plants

SEAL SALAMANDER
(DESMOGNATHUS MONTICOLA)

Seal salamanders are mostly aquatic but spend some time on land. They are lungless salamanders that breathe through their skin. Well-developed feet help seal salamanders move along the pebbles and rocks of fast-moving water. They usually hide under rocks during the day and are active at night. Seal salamanders have light-brown to gray backs and dark-brown patterned markings. Their undersides are white, and their tails narrow to a sharp edge at the tip.

HOW TO SPOT

Size: 3.3 to 5 inches (8.4 to 12.7 cm) long
Range: Appalachian Mountains
Habitat: Clear springs and smaller streams in forests
Diet: Small aquatic insects and other invertebrates such as worms

FUN FACT
Seal salamanders get their name from the way they hold their heads up, similar to the way a seal sits.

SALAMANDERS

SIBERIAN SALAMANDER
(SALAMANDRELLA KEYSERLINGII)

Siberian salamanders are the only species of salamander that live in the Arctic Circle. They have mostly smooth skin with bumps along their sides. Their tails are flat, and the tails are usually shorter than their bodies. Siberian salamander bodies are brown, bronze, olive, or grayish. They can have silver bands going down their backs and dark spots. Siberian salamanders hide under shelters during the day and are mainly active at night.

HOW TO SPOT

Size: 3.5 to 4.9 inches (9 to 12.5 cm) long
Range: Northeast Asia
Habitat: Forests with swamps, rivers, and lakes
Diet: Earthworms, insects, mollusks, and other invertebrates

COLD AS ICE

Siberian salamanders face extremely cold arctic temperatures. To survive, they replace the water in their bodies with special chemicals that prevent them from freezing. They are known for their ability to survive in a frozen state under the ice for several years and thaw when the ice melts.

SPLENDID MOROCCAN SALAMANDER
(SALAMANDRA ALGIRA SPLENDENS)

Splendid Moroccan salamanders are a subspecies of North African fire salamanders. They have black bodies with bright-yellow and red patches. Red patches are usually on the neck, but they can also be on the tail and body. Splendid Moroccan salamanders have long, flat heads and slim bodies. They are nocturnal and spend their days hiding under logs, dead trees, or stones, or even in rodent burrows.

HOW TO SPOT

Size: 8.5 inches (21.5 cm) long
Range: Western and central Rif Mountains in Morocco
Habitat: Mountain forests, shrublands near brooks and streams, and caves
Diet: Invertebrates

FUN FACT
Splendens in the scientific name refers to the salamander's bright, splendid colors.

SALAMANDERS

TIGER SALAMANDER
(AMBYSTOMA TIGRINUM)

Tiger salamanders are the largest land-dwelling salamanders in North America. They also have the largest geographic range of any North American salamander. Tiger salamanders are dark with yellow, tan, or olive spots or stripes. Their undersides are yellow or olive. Their bodies are thick, with smooth skin that is moist and shiny. They have large heads with wide, round snouts and round eyes. The texture and thickness of their skin allows them to survive on land, but they need to burrow underground to get enough moisture.

FUN FACT
Tiger salamanders have been found as deep as 2 feet (0.6 m) underground.

HOW TO SPOT

Size: 7 to 14 inches (17.8 to 35.6 cm) long
Range: United States, Canada, and Mexico
Habitat: Forests near ponds, lakes, slow-moving streams, and fresh pools
Diet: Worms, snails, insects, and slugs

TWO-TOED AMPHIUMA
(AMPHIUMA MEANS)

Two-toed amphiumas range from brown to dark gray to nearly black. They have large, cylindrical bodies. Their eyes and limbs are very small, and each leg has two toes, giving them their name. Because of their tiny legs and snake-like movements, they are often called Congo eels. Juveniles are born with gills but lose them early in their development. Two-toed amphiumas are long, slippery, and completely aquatic, but they can occasionally be found on land during rainstorms. They have strong jaws and sharp teeth that they use to catch and eat prey.

HOW TO SPOT

Size: 3 to 4 feet (0.9 to 1.2 m) long
Range: Southeastern United States
Habitat: Swamps, ponds, and other still waters
Diet: Fish, frogs, crayfish, and small snakes

NEWTS

ALGERIAN RIBBED NEWT
(PLEURODELES NEBULOSUS)

The Algerian ribbed newt is a medium-sized salamander. It has a wide, flat head, a flattened body, and a rounded snout. Algerian ribbed newts are brown with a greenish or yellowish tint and dark, uneven spots. Their heads, backs, and tails have small yellow or brown dots, and their sides are yellowish. Their undersides are pale gray and usually have dark-brown, round spots. Males have tails that are longer than their bodies, and females have shorter tails. When they enter the water during breeding season, Algerian ribbed newts develop fins along their backs and their undersides.

FUN FACT
Algerian ribbed newts were once considered a vulnerable species. But they have been protected in Tunisia since 2006. Although there are still threats in some areas, the species' population is considered stable.

HOW TO SPOT

Size: 7.1 inches (18 cm) long on average but can be up to 11 inches (28 cm) long
Range: Algeria and Tunisia
Habitat: Rivers, ponds, swamps, and pools of water
Diet: Invertebrates and small fish

CALIFORNIA NEWT *(TARICHA TOROSA)*

California newts are active both during the day and at night. They live primarily on land. They become aquatic during breeding season, which is usually between December and May. They have sturdy, medium-sized bodies with rough, warty skin on their backs. They vary in color from yellowish brown to dark brown and have pale-yellow to orange undersides. They have large eyes that stick out from their heads. Adults are toxic, and if they are attacked, they will release that toxin, causing death or paralysis in predators.

HOW TO SPOT

Size: 4.9 to 7.9 inches (12.5 to 20 cm) long
Range: California mountains
Habitat: Northern population likes moist forests; southern population prefers dry forests
Diet: Small invertebrates such as worms, snails, slugs, and sowbugs; insects; and amphibian eggs and larvae

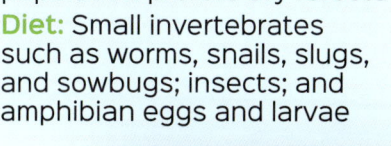

FIGHTING WILDFIRES

California newts have a special defense against wildfires. They have a coating on their skin that foams up and turns to crusty, white ash that protects them from catching fire. The foam seals underneath the ash, shielding them from the heat of the fire.

NEWTS

CHINESE WARTY NEWT
(PARAMESOTRITON CHINENSIS)

Chinese warty newts have rough, warty skin and short, round bodies. Their skin varies in color from light gray to olive to dark brown. Sometimes they have yellow or orange stripes down the middle of their backs. Others may have black, brown, or olive spots and marks. Chinese warty newts have small yellow or orange spots on their sides and backs. Their undersides are bluish black with yellow or orange-red spots up to the throat. The lower edge of their tails are yellowish red with dark spots. Females have black-tipped tails. Male tails have a pearly blue shine on the sides.

HOW TO SPOT

Size: 6.3 inches (16 cm) long
Range: Central China
Habitat: Marshy areas of tropical and subtropical forests
Diet: Invertebrates

Female

EASTERN NEWT
(NOTOPHTHALMUS VIRIDESCENS)

Eastern newts are one of the few species in the true salamander family that are native to North America. They go through metamorphosis as they develop. Eastern newts start life as larvae with feathery gills. Then the juvenile stage generally lasts from two to three years. During this time, they are called efts. Efts have dry, rough skin and can be bright orange, dull red, or brownish with light spots. Efts live fully on land and are highly toxic. Adult eastern newts are aquatic, returning to the water. Adults are olive green with black-ringed red spots on their backs.

HOW TO SPOT

Size: 2.8 to 4.9 inches (7 to 12.4 cm) long

Range: Eastern North America

Habitat: Small bodies of fresh water with mud bottoms in forests

Diet: Adults eat any small invertebrate that they can find, as well as tadpoles

Adult

FUN FACT

Eastern newts have a lot of variation in their life cycles depending on the environment. Some populations go straight from larva to adult, skipping the eft stage. Some never leave the eft stage, and some keep their larval features as adults.

Eft

NEWTS

GREAT CRESTED NEWT
(TRITURUS CRISTATUS)

Great crested newts are also called warty newts. They are best known for the large crest of skin that develops on the male's back. Males also have a white stripe on the end of the tail. Great crested newts have dark-brown or black warty skin on their backs, and some of the warts have white tips that look like spots. Their undersides are orange with uneven patterns of black spots. Great crested newts are active at night and spend most of their time near water to keep their skin moist.

FUN FACT
A great crested newt's underside pattern is like a human fingerprint. Each pattern is different.

Male

HOW TO SPOT

Size: 3.9 to 5.5 inches (10 to 14 cm) long
Range: Western Europe through the United Kingdom
Habitat: Forests, glades, bushlands, woodlands, marshes, pastures, and parks and gardens
Diet: Worms, slugs, insects, mollusks, and tadpoles

HIMALAYAN NEWT
(TYLOTOTRITON VERRUCOSUS)

Himalayan newts are also known as crocodile newts. They are chocolate brown or black and have orange or orange-brown bumps along their ribs. The tail is flattened with a fin fold. The tail is a lighter color than the body. Himalayan newts spend spring, summer, and fall in the water. During the winter, they burrow underground. Himalayan newts are considered bad luck in Myanmar and are often killed or used to catch fish.

HOW TO SPOT

Size: 6.3 to 7.9 inches (16 to 20 cm) long
Range: China, India, Myanmar, Nepal, and Thailand
Habitat: Mountain forests, shrublands, and wetlands
Diet: Invertebrates such as insects and earthworms

NEWTS

LORESTAN NEWT
(NEURERGUS KAISERI)

Lorestan newts are also known as Kaiser mountain newts. They get their name from the area where they are found. The back is black with white spots and a narrow orange, red, or yellow stripe from behind the head to the tail. Lorestan newts have orange-red or white undersides with black markings, and their legs have white, orange-red, and black marks. They have large eyes that they can use both in and out of water. Lorestan newts are critically endangered because of their limited range and habitat loss. They are also captured and sold as pets.

HOW TO SPOT

Size: 3.9 to 5.5 inches (9.9 to 14 cm) long

Range: Southern Zagros Mountains in the Lorestan province of Iran

Habitat: Small, slow parts of streams with rocky or sandy bottoms; and open woodlands

Diet: Small invertebrates

FUN FACT
The geographic range of Lorestan newts is extremely small. They occupy four streams within a 3.9-square-mile (10 sq km) radius in the Zagros Mountains.

ROUGH-SKINNED NEWT
(TARICHA GRANULOSA)

Rough-skinned newts are named for the rough, pebbly skin on their backs. They are dark brown to gray on top and have bright yellow-orange undersides. Rough-skinned newts live on land but return to the water to breed. Some rough-skinned newts will spend their entire lives in the water. Those living in lakes or ponds will spend the winter in the water and stay active for most of the season. Those living on land or in shallow water hibernate on land in rock openings or under rotting logs.

HOW TO SPOT

Size: 5 to 8.5 inches (12.7 to 21.6 cm) long
Range: Pacific Coast of North America
Habitat: Forested areas near slow or still bodies of water
Diet: Insects, slugs, worms, and amphibian eggs and larvae

DEADLY!

Rough-skinned newts are the most poisonous amphibians in the Pacific Northwest. One newt has enough poison to kill 25,000 mice. The garter snake has developed an immunity to the newt's poison and is its only true predator.

NEWTS

SMOOTH NEWT *(LISSOTRITON VULGARIS)*

Smooth newts have smooth olive or pale-brown skin with dark spots on their throats. They have orange undersides with black spots. Females are paler than males, and males are longer. Males develop a crest that runs from head to tail during breeding season, and their orange bellies become brighter. While the larvae are growing, they will shed their skin around once a week. They do not become adults until they are about three years old.

HOW TO SPOT

Size: 3.1 to 4.3 inches (8 to 11 cm) long
Range: Europe, including British Isles, into western Asia
Habitat: Swamps, woodlands, parks, gardens, wet moorlands, marshes, and farmlands
Diet: Insects, slugs, worms, tadpoles, water snails, and small crustaceans such as shrimp

FUN FACT
On land, smooth newts catch prey by sticking out their tongues. In the water, they use their teeth.

SPANISH NEWT (PLEURODELES WALTL)

Spanish newts are also known as sharp-ribbed newts or Iberian newts. They are entirely aquatic and only leave their ponds in search of new habitats. Spanish newts have flat bodies. This helps them slip under logs and rocks. They are covered in small warts and have dark-brown skin with dark-brown spots across their sides. Dull orange circles run down their sides where their ribs stick out. Spanish newts prefer slow-moving water such as ponds because they are poor swimmers.

HOW TO SPOT

Size: 5.9 to 11.8 inches (15 to 30 cm) long
Range: Portugal, Spain, and northern Morocco
Habitat: Ponds and lagoons in scrublands and woodlands
Diet: Invertebrates and small fish

FROM RIBS TO SWORDS

Spanish newts have a fascinating way of defending themselves from predators. They can push their ribs out through pores in their skin, releasing poison. The tips stick out of their bodies like poisonous spikes. If predators are punctured, it can cause them pain or death. Spanish newts can also release poison from glands at the backs of their heads and on their tails.

CAECILIANS

CONGO CAECILIAN
(HERPELE SQUALOSTOMA)

Congo caecilians have purplish-gray bodies. Their snouts stick out, but they have no visible eyes. They have tentacles close to their nostrils that push in and out. They use their tentacles to check out their environment and find prey. Little is known about their behavior, but like other African caecilians, scientists believe they are fossorial, or burrowing, creatures.

HOW TO SPOT

Size: 16 inches (40.6 cm) long
Range: Central and western Africa
Habitat: Lowland forests, living mostly underground
Diet: Termites, earthworms, ants, and other life-forms that live in soil

FUN FACT
Congo caecilian mothers have an interesting way of caring for their young. Their skin is filled with nutrients, and the babies bite off the outer layer with their teeth. This behavior is called dermatophagy.

KIRK'S CAECILIAN
(SCOLECOMORPHUS KIRKII)

Kirk's caecilians have 130 to 152 rings around their bodies. Their skin is purplish gray with a cream-colored underside. The top and sides of their heads are a similar color to the rest of their bodies, except for a light area near their tentacles. The tentacles are found on the sides of the snout underneath their nostrils, and they line up with the front of their mouths. Their eyes are on the tentacles. This means the eyes can move out from the skull. Kirk's caecilians burrow in soil and piles of fallen leaves, twigs, and bark.

HOW TO SPOT

Size: 8.5 to 18.2 inches (21.5 to 46.3 cm) long
Range: Tanzania, Malawi, and Mozambique
Habitat: Tropical rain forests and farming areas in mountainous regions
Diet: Invertebrates and soil

CAECILIANS

RINGED CAECILIAN
(SIPHONOPS ANNULATUS)

Ringed caecilians are a species in the family of South American caecilians. They have cylindrical, shiny, blue-black bodies with white rings. Males and females are similar in appearance most of the time, but the female will turn a whitish-blue color when she's caring for young. Ringed caecilians spend most of their time in underground burrows that they dig. Their tentacles help them find their way through the underground areas.

HOW TO SPOT

Size: 11.3 to 17.7 inches (28.6 to 45 cm) long

Range: Argentina, Bolivia, Brazil, Colombia, Ecuador, French Guiana, Peru, and Venezuela

Habitat: Humid soil in forested and open environments

Diet: Earthworms, termites, crickets, slugs, snails, and other invertebrates that live in soil

RIO CAUCA CAECILIAN
(TYPHLONECTES NATANS)

Rio Cauca caecilians are a species of aquatic caecilians. They spend most of their lives in water and are rarely found on land. Their bodies are flat with a small tail fin, and they are often confused with eels. They are dark grayish black, and their mouths are hidden underneath their long snouts. They can tell the difference between light and dark. But they are otherwise blind. Tentacles located near their eyes and nostrils help them find food and sense predators. Rio Cauca caecilians have lungs, but they primarily breathe by absorbing oxygen from the water through their skin.

HOW TO SPOT

Size: 17 to 22 inches (43.2 to 55.9 cm) long

Range: Colombia and Venezuela

Habitat: Rivers, marshes, and lakes

Diet: Invertebrates such as insects, worms, and spiders

FUN FACT

In 2019, a Rio Cauca caecilian found in Florida became the first recorded caecilian in North America. Experts think a pet owner dumped the caecilian into a canal.

GLOSSARY

arachnid
A class of animals that includes spiders, scorpions, mites, and ticks.

camouflage
To hide by blending in.

cloaca
A chamber from which excretory and reproductive materials are released in animals such as amphibians, reptiles, and birds.

crustacean
A water animal such as a crab that has jointed sections and a tough outer shell.

ecosystem
A community of interacting organisms and their environment.

evolve
Develop gradually.

hibernate
To become inactive or sleep during the winter.

invertebrate
An animal without a backbone or a bony skeleton.

larva
An early form of an animal.

mangrove
Trees or bushes that grow in thick bunches in salty water.

predator
An animal that survives by killing and eating other animals.

prey
An animal that is hunted or killed by other animals for food.

vent
The anus of an amphibian and other animals.

TO LEARN MORE

FURTHER READINGS

King, Ernest. *Reptiles and Amphibians: An Augmented Reality Popup Book*. Far Sight, 2019.

Pearson, Marie. *Essential Amphibians*. Abdo, 2021.

ONLINE RESOURCES

To learn more about amphibians, please visit **abdobooklinks.com** or scan this QR code. These links are routinely monitored and updated to provide the most current information available.

PHOTO CREDITS

Cover Photos: Dirk Ercken/Shutterstock Images, front (dyeing poison dart frog); Gary Powell/Shutterstock Images, front (eastern red-spotted newt); Lev Frid/Shutterstock Images, front (glass frog); Hintau Aliaksei/Shutterstock Images, front (marsh frog); Michiel de Wit/Shutterstock Images, front (northern leopard frog); Peterr R./Shutterstock Images, front (red-eyed tree frog); Dirk Ercken/Shutterstock Images, front (strawberry poison frog;) Robert Eastman/Shutterstock Images, front (tiger salamander); Kurit afshen/Shutterstock Images, front (flying tree frogs); Eric Isselee/Shutterstock Images, back (axolotl); Vitalii Hulai/Shutterstock Images, back (common frog)

Interior Photos: Alex Stemmers/Shutterstock Images, 1 (top left), 13 (left), 13 (right), 24, 112 (center); Rosa Jay/Shutterstock Images, 1 (top right), 5 (top left), 31 (bottom), 42 (bottom), 48, 93; Shutterstock Images, 1 (bottom left), 6 (bottom), 11, 20 (bottom), 22 (bottom), 25 (left), 42 (top), 44 (top), 44 (bottom), 50 (top), 60 (top), 66 (bottom), 91, 94, 95 (top), 95 (bottom), 101 (top), 101 (bottom), 112 (top left), 112 (bottom left); Dante Fenolio/Science Source, 1 (left center), 12, 63 (top), 80, 86 (bottom), 100, 104, 106, 112 (right); Patrick K. Campbell/Shutterstock Images, 1 (bottom right), 5 (bottom right), 58; Sergio Gutierrez Getino/Shutterstock Images, 4 (top), 71 (top); Mariska Boertjens/Shutterstock Images, 4 (bottom left), 46 (top); Tanes Ngamsom/iStockphoto, 4 (bottom center), 99 (top); Greg Dimijian/Science Source, 4 (bottom right), 17 (bottom); Marco Maggesi/Shutterstock Images, 5 (top center), 76; Eric Isselle/Shutterstock Images, 5 (top right), 51 (bottom); James DeBoer/Shutterstock Images, 5 (bottom left), 92 (top); Maximillian cabinet/Shutterstock Images, 6 (top), 66 (top); Fundación Atelopus, 7, 67; Kaan Sezer/iStockphoto, 8; iStockphoto, 9, 87 (top); Henri Koskinen/Shutterstock Images, 10 (top); Hintau Aliaksei/Shutterstock Images, 10 (bottom); Ken Griffiths/Shutterstock Images, 14, 19, 28, 50 (bottom); Michael Benard/Shutterstock Images, 15 (left), 15 (right), 16 (bottom), 33, 54, 97 (top); Jay Ondreicka/Shutterstock Images, 16 (top), 97 (bottom); David Havel/Shutterstock Images, 17 (top); Toshikazu Sato/Yomiuri Shimbun/AP Images, 18; Daniel Heuclin/Bios Photo/Science Source, 20 (top); Gregory G. Dimijian/Science Source, 21; NHPA/Photo Shot/Science Source, 22 (top), 39; Melinda Fawver/Shutterstock Images, 23 (top), 85 (top); Luna Summer/Shutterstock Images, 23 (bottom); Paul Starosta/Getty Images, 25 (right); John Serrao/Science Source, 26, 89; Thulung Photo/Shutterstock Images, 27 (top); Reality Images/Shutterstock Images, 27 (bottom);

Philippe Clement/Shutterstock Images, 29; Pablo Méndez/Age Foto Stock/Alamy, 30 (top); Pedro Luna/Shutterstock Images, 30 (bottom), 62 (bottom); Juan Aceituno/Shutterstock Images, 31 (top); Brian Lasenby/Shutterstock Images, 32; Stephen Dalton/Science Source, 34 (top), 52; Michiel de Wit/Shutterstock Images, 34 (bottom), 78 (right); Kirsanov Valeriy Vladimirovich/Shutterstock Images, 35; Karl H. Switak/Science Source, 36 (left), 72; Jeffrey B. Banke/Shutterstock Images, 36 (right); Suzanne L. Collins/Science Source, 37, 38; K. Jayaram/Science Source, 40; Vaclav Sebek/Shutterstock Images, 41 (top); Ryan M. Bolton/Alamy, 41 (bottom); Ryan M. Bolton/Shutterstock Images, 43 (top), 86 (top); Dr. Morley Read/Shutterstock Images, 43 (bottom); Marty Crump, 45; Dirk Ercken/Shutterstock Images, 46 (bottom); Mark Smith/Science Source, 47; ANT Photo Library/Science Source, 49; Dave M. Hunt Photography/Shutterstock Images, 51 (top); Bocky Tandiono/iStockphoto, 53; Rudmer Zwerver/Shutterstock Images, 55 (top), 102; Cezary Korkosz/Shutterstock Images, 55 (bottom); Alan B. Schroeder/Shutterstock Images, 56; Les Palenik/Shutterstock Images, 57; E. R. Degginger/Science Source, 59, 74; Jane Rix/Shutterstock Images, 60 (bottom); Valt Ahyppo/Shutterstock Images, 61; Marek R. Swadzba/Shutterstock Images, 62 (top); K. Hanley CHD Photo/Shutterstock Images, 63 (bottom); Matt Jeppson/Shutterstock Images, 64; Ch'ien Lee/Minden Pictures/SuperStock, 65; Hurly D'souza/Shutterstock Images, 68; Stuart Wilson/Science Source, 69; Andreas Zerndl/Shutterstock Images, 70; Kazakov Maksim/Shutterstock Images, 71 (bottom); Tristan Tan/Shutterstock Images, 73; Animals Animals/SuperStock, 75; Jacob Loyacano/Shutterstock Images, 77; Hunter Kauffman/Shutterstock Images, 78 (left); Federico Crovetto/Shutterstock Images, 79; Tania Araujo/iStockphoto, 81; Robert J. Erwin/Science Source, 82; Joseph T. Collins/Science Source, 83; Martin Voeller/iStockphoto, 84; Eva B./Shutterstock Images, 85 (bottom); Francesco Tomasinelli/Science Source, 87 (bottom); Bryce Wade/CalPhotos, 88; Miroslav Hlavko/Shutterstock Images, 90; Lauren Suryanata/Shutterstock Images, 92 (bottom); Wirestock Creators/Shutterstock Images, 96; Mike Lane 45/iStockphoto, 98; Poring Studio/Shutterstock Images, 99 (bottom); Vitalii Hulai/Shutterstock Images, 103; Joachim Nerz/CalPhoto, 105 (top), 105 (bottom); Nature's Images/Science Source, 107

ABDOBOOKS.COM
Published by Abdo Publishing, a division of ABDO, PO Box 398166, Minneapolis, Minnesota 55439. Copyright © 2023 by Abdo Consulting Group, Inc. International copyrights reserved in all countries. No part of this book may be reproduced in any form without written permission from the publisher. Abdo Reference™ is a trademark and logo of Abdo Publishing.

Printed in the United States of America, North Mankato, Minnesota.
052022
092022

THIS BOOK CONTAINS RECYCLED MATERIALS

Editor: Katharine Hale
Series Designer: Colleen McLaren
Content Consultant: Martha L. (Marty) Crump, PhD; Adjunct Professor, Utah State University and Northern Arizona University

Library of Congress Control Number: 2021952336
Publisher's Cataloging-in-Publication Data
Names: Seigel, Rachel, author.
Title: Amphibians / by Rachel Seigel
Description: Minneapolis, Minnesota : Abdo Publishing, 2023 | Series: Field guides | Includes online resources and index.
Identifiers: ISBN 9781532198793 (lib. bdg.) | ISBN 9781098272449 (ebook)
Subjects: LCSH: Amphibians--Juvenile literature. | Amphibians--Behavior--Juvenile literature. | Animals--Identification--Juvenile literature. | Zoology--Juvenile literature.
Classification: DDC 597.8--dc23

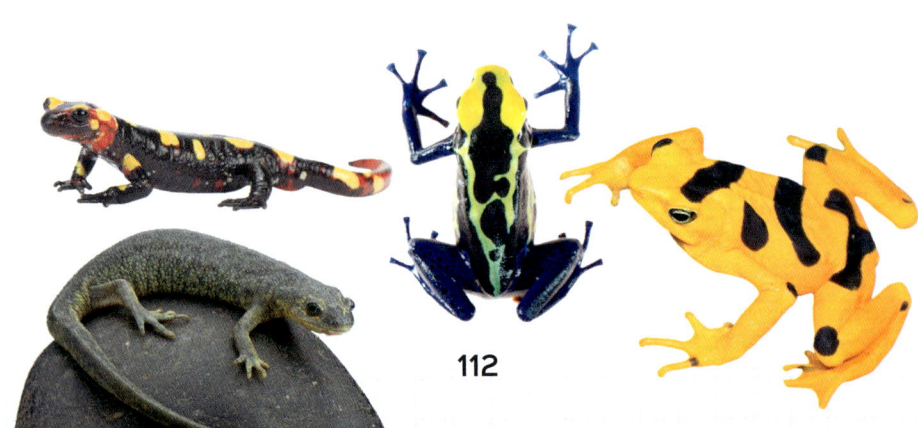